September 18, 1967, I woke up to the sad, life changing news that my mom had died during the night. She was 36 years old. I had just turned 15 years old in August, and my sister Marilyn had turned 12 years in January of that same year.

My mom had been sick with Lupus for many years, and it had a devastating effect on her kidneys. She was receiving kidney dialysis three times a week. In the 60's I don't believe that kidney transplants were performed. Kidney dialysis was being used, but this was a new treatment for kidney failure. My mother had her dialysis shunt connected to her veins, sometimes in her arm, sometimes her leg, but the actual shunt was not under the skin. It was outside of the body. You could see the blood flowing through the shunt. Quite a few times, my mom would look at her shunt and become very concerned. She could actually see the blood clotting inside of the tubing. When this would happen, she would have to go back to the hospital and have the shunt moved to a new location. My mom was understandably upset, but it didn't last for long. She would come home and go back to being her wonderful faith-filled positive self. How she did this, I do not know. I am sure it had to do with her deep faith in God.

At 15 years old, I did not realize what a strong impact the loss of my mother would have on my life. I never got to know her as a person or friend. I could not go to her for motherly advice when I had my own children. When I had hard decisions in my life that I would have liked to talk with my mother about, I felt cheated. Maybe the greatest loss was not having someone that loved me unconditionally, as only a mother can. I also felt bad for my children because they missed out on having a wonderful woman like my mother as their grandmother.

I remember my mother as a wonderful woman, but only as I grew older did I really appreciate what a unique individual she was. My mother was always smiling. Okay, maybe not always, but 98% of the time. This was remarkable, considering she suffered from her illness and knew she didn't have a long life ahead of her. She once said to a friend, "I hope I can live long enough to see my daughters grow up." Even though I think she knew that, she probably would not.

I Love

Lola

SUE SOBIN

Blossom
Book Publishing
A Division of Blossom Marketing & Publishing, LLC

Published by Blossom Book Publishing
Medina, Ohio

Printed in the United States of America

When she would greet people and ask how they were, she REALLY wanted to know. It was not just a routine question that we all seem to ask. I can see her now, giving the person her undivided attention with a caring look in her beautiful brown eyes and a smile on her lovely face. Years after my mother died, when I would visit my father, who lived on the same street that I grew up on. I would routinely take a walk down the street. If I happened to meet one of the neighbors, without a doubt, they would bring up my mother and remark on what a wonderful woman she was. This was years after her death. That is the impression she imprinted on people with her lovely personality.

As I continued to get older and reflect on memories of my mother and her life, I truly realized what a deep loss it was not to have her in my life.

One day, I asked my father if he would be willing to write down some things about my mom, so I could "get to know her" a little better. I remembered that she was a wonderful, loving woman that was always smiling. However, I wanted more. I did not know what exactly, but I knew I needed to know more about her.

My father came through in flying colors. He wrote a memoir about my mother that is just beautiful and filled with love. He asked me if I would like to have something written down about his life too. Of course, I wanted these precious documents. Again, he did not disappoint but wrote a wonderful memoir about his life.

This book is a combination of these two writings. They show courage, a deep faith in God, and a beautiful pure love between a man and a woman.

The following are my father's memories and, in my opinion, his tribute to a very special lady.

To Susan:

I have been searching my mind for facts that may be of interest to you and your sister. Please appreciate that it has taken many months to compile this summary. Yet it is well worth it and had each generation done this in my ancestry; it would have been fascinating to read about my generation's past. Anyway, I think so.

Several times in the past, it has been mentioned that you would like to know more about your mother. I decided to write an account of this so you can have this written account to refer to from time to time. Perhaps sometime in the future, your children will find it of benefit as well, and it may be helpful in other aspects. As I reflect on this, it would have been of great importance to me had my ancestors done the same. I am sure that we would all be interested in our bloodlines. In an account such as this, however, the acts should be presented in the most factual way so that a true account of the history of the person can be presented for a true concept. With this thought in mind, the following paragraphs will follow this vein. In some instances, when I deviate from this factual report, I shall qualify the reports as "in my opinion" or in a manner to allow you to draw your own conclusions.

Lola Fedor, born of Emily and Walter Fedorowitz, was delivered by caesarian section. She was the only child of Walter and Emily. Emily had a brother named Stanley Robak, who resided in Detroit, Michigan. Stanley was of short stature, had gray wavy hair, and was trim in figure. He impressed me as possessing a sort of quiet dignity. A man of apparent dignity, he was employed by the Chrysler Corporation and held the position of superintendent. He drove a big black Chrysler and smoked good cigars. I was impressed by his manner and kindness, and generosity. You, Susan, would not remember him, but he was very fond of you and once insisted on pushing you around in a baby wheeler at Cedar Point. He passed away from a heart attack and other complications. His fondness for Lola was expressed in his will when he left her $6,500.00 in cash after his death. Money at that time had more value. This can be compared to the prices at that time since I purchased our home, where this is being written, for $11,500.00. Emily and Stanley also talked of a brother who was still in Poland whose name was Bolek. He was a victim of the war, and they lost track of him. The war I refer to here is the Second World War.

Emily was of Polish extraction. In her younger days, she was very pleasant with a good personality, which at times erupted as a volcano would and certainly indicated she was not entirely passive in her personality. Her statue was of the short variety but well endowed. It was a tribute to God that He could pack all of that into such a small package without her being short-changed.

The relationship between Walter and Emily was not of the best variety, and there were many differences between them that became explosive. Some of this could be attributed to Walter's physical condition, which involved a kidney disorder that caused him to be irritable at times. This is not to take away from a man who supported his family and had a lot of love for his wife and daughter.

Walter himself was a unique personality. He was gray with a lot of hair and a pleasant expression on his face as if it were in a continual smile. Walter Fedor was a veteran of the First World War. His religious beliefs were not too evident, but at times he could quote scriptures at random. He worked at a factory located at or in the area of (between Fleet and Harvard) off Broadway Avenue. It was a place that used heavy hammers that impaired his hearing. Walter was of Russian extraction but spoke Polish of a sort. This, coupled with a Russian accent, made it somewhat difficult to understand him at times.

Walter's death was due to a ruptured vein in his lung, which burst, and he poured blood from his mouth. He was in the veteran's hospital at this time and died there. The government paid all of the funeral expenses, coffin, plot, marker, etc. To the best of my knowledge, he is buried at Hillcrest cemetery. This location is rather dim to me at the moment, but it is not in Cleveland. This sums up the knowledge of Walter at the moment. You may wish to ask me questions later about him, which you can do.

Emily Fedor had a cousin in Jackson, Michigan. Her name was Mary Cierwiec. She was about the same age as Emily, and they referred to each other as "sisters." Their relationship was such that they had their differences that sometimes erupted in stormy sessions. On occasion, we would visit Mary in Jackson, Michigan. On one of these occasions, we met some of her friends. These friends were Loretta and Van Spansky. Loretta's mother and father were Mary's first acquaintances. Loretta knew them as a very small child who eventually grew into the relationship through the years. Van became a part of it when he married Loretta. We became good friends and continued to visit them after Mary's death.

This brief background has importance since you now know some of your family histories. I shall now proceed to tell you about your mother, Lola Constance Fedor (short for Federowitz.) She was an only child, born by caesarian section. Apparently, her mother or her father were not practicing Catholics since Lola was not baptized until she was sixteen. She took religious instructions and practiced her faith with dedication.

My introduction to her came about on a summer evening while I tended the Bakery Store. The first such occasion happened when she came in with her mother to purchase baked goods. Yes, I did notice her right away and particularly noticed her flowing brown hair. She would come into the store on several occasions with her mother and just a couple of times by herself. Then only her mother would come in after that, and I started to inquire as to the whereabouts of her daughter. Her mother said it was permissible to stop in and see her if I wished, but she was going to high school, South High School, and was very busy. Shortly after that, I found myself making my way to her home, which was located one block up from the bakery in a two-story dwelling, upstairs, on Mound Avenue, of which they rented the upstairs apartment. Our first meeting was pleasurable, but I must have annoyed her in some way or another throughout the evening since I remember her hitting me on the head with a checkered board. The board was made of cardboard, not wood. She wasn't that mad. We started to keep company after that, and we build a good friendship.

During this time, I would drive her about or perform errands for her mother and father. I was also able to console Lola when her father was in St. Alexis hospital desperately ill, and it appeared to be the end. He received the Last Rites while he was unconscious, but he must have been aware of the last rites because he announced quite vigorously that he was not checking out yet.

Your mother asked me if I would be interested in taking her to the prom, and I agreed. She asked me if I had a friend who would take her friend also. I had in mind my cousin Ray, but being an older fellow, we said we would have to see the girl first. This was arranged, and the girl was very attractive, and Ray leaped at the chance to take her to the prom. Ray and I thought we were just going along for the ride mainly and really didn't take the situation seriously. The prom was at the Tudor Arms Hotel. We began spending our time at the bar, but this came to an abrupt end, initiated by your mother, as she approached the bar and stated flatly, but not lacking in vigor, "Did you come here to drink, or did you come here with us?" We got the message and spent the rest of the evening with them.

We continued to see each other after this, but I always felt that I was too old for your mother. There was a very pronounced difference in our ages – an eleven-year difference. Yet, she did not feel this way, as I found out rather abruptly one afternoon while we drove on Broadway Avenue. The conversation got around to our relationship, and as I hedged, she came out very bluntly and asked, "Well, are we going steady or not?" My answer related to our age difference, and she said there was absolutely no reason for this to impair our relationship at all. It was then that we started dating seriously, and I'll admit that I had visions in the back of my mind of marriage. I had dated many girls but had rarely thought seriously of being married to them, except in a couple of cases, but this is not prevalent to this writing.

As we dated, I noticed she had a charm and a maturity beyond her seventeen years. We had many things in common and enjoyed each other's company. This is not to say that there weren't some differences, and sometimes our differences bordered on the explosive. Yet, paradoxically, when we married, many of these differences melted away. But this puts me ahead of the story, so let us back up and relate some of our dating experiences so you may have a better knowledge of your mother's nature and personal make-up.

Television had not been invented or rather was in its initial stages of infancy. Each Sunday night, there was a radio program on at about 11:00 p.m. called "Ghost Stories." We made it a point to listen to this program without fail. Her mother and father had gone to bed, and Lola and I would be cuddled up on the couch, supposedly shaking with fear and protecting each other. My personal observation of this was that it was great, and the stories too were well done and did carry an element of apprehension capable of raising the blood pressure to a degree. The most gratifying thing about it all was that her parents exhibited real trust in me since they left us alone.

According to your mother, I was the first boy who was accorded this type of trust. All the others were continually being screened by her father. This amazed her, and she let me know that I should be honored that they showed such trust. At my age, I truly realize the profundity of this even more. Since being a father, I have experienced these same protective feelings. So, we continued to date and did what dating boys and girls do.

There were movies and dances and amusement parks, but significantly all of these things were meaningful only because we were together enjoying each other's company. At times we had limited times together since your mother was occupied with other activities. One of these was a part-time job for a dentist Dr. Potylicki. Her capacity was as a dental assistant and receptionist. This is how it came about that Dr. Polyliucki became Marilyn's godfather. She was good at her job, very good. In fact, since her personality was pleasant and cheerful and she was sensitive to the need of the patients.

We spent many Sunday afternoons out in the country. Mantua, in fact, or Streetsboro, which is so close, they are interrelated. Lola's father had a Russian friend he would visit out there. This man's last name was March, who professed that he was a communist. His occupation was tending beehives and selling honey for profit. His wife Irene, who was considerably younger, was charming and had a striking resemblance to Elizabeth, the queen of England. They had a son named Roland, and Irene's father lived with them also. The boy was very young at the time, about four years old, and on many occasions, I would take him out to the variety store for an ice cream treat. I bring this out simply because he is a grown man now, works at Broadhead & Garrett, and happens to be Mike's boss.

The grandfather was hunched over but was continually working at something diligently. I mention him too because he taught me lessons in tenacity simply by powers of example. One incident specifically that made a profound impression on me was that he had cut his hand, all the way across his palm, with a ten-inch circular saw. It was heavily bandaged, but he continued to do his work in spite of it. When I asked him about the pain, he admitted that it did hurt, but he said he couldn't feel sorry for himself and his work must continue.

School plays was another activity that kept Lola occupied at times. I know of two specifically that she acted in, and one play where she played the character "Penny," short for Penelope. It was a very extensive part. Since I took up much of her time, she was pressed for study time for this part. Many times, she would say that I couldn't come over that night since she had to memorize the role, but somehow, I would end up there anyway. As a result, it really boiled down to the last time to study was the night before the play. The following evening, I asked her how the play went, and she said, "Fine" even though she had to learn all of the rest of the part the night before. This was very impressive since I had a hard time memorizing "Mary Had A Little Lamb" when I was a kid.

I am attempting to add these little anecdotes so that you may yourself determine the nature, personality, and character of your mother. I hope to, through some of these little incidents or stories, enable you to draw your own conclusions and perhaps even understand a lot better simply because of your femininity. Lola was a very good person and definitely human.

Previously I had mentioned the March's and our frequent visits to their farm in Streetsboro. It was a beautiful place to visit in the summertime, but our visiting there was not restricted by the seasons. I recall a particular visit we made on one winter evening with the snow falling gently. As we pulled into their drive, Lola's mother and father went inside. Lola lingered until I got out of the car and then started to assault me with a barrage of snowballs. I used the straightforward attack and rushed right in, scooped a fresh handful of snow, and promptly washed her face with it thoroughly and convincingly. She offered no resistance but instead looked right into my eyes like a defenseless little lamb. Of course, at that moment, I scooped her up and crushed her to me. That kiss and hug was "cool man" and very memorial as a very pleasant moment – vintage classification.

When Lola and I met, she was seventeen years old, as was mentioned. We had an unwritten understanding after dating for a while that we would marry. It was also understood that she would first finish high school, which really ended up in a three-year courtship since she was twenty when I married her. This is not to infer that she was 20 when she finished high school. I know that she had finished school long before that. It may have been that she wanted to work for a while and make some money to buy the things she needed because after we were married, I don't recall her working much after that.

Another story I can relate in regard to your mother's personality and tastes was her selection of finer entertainment. One evening as I was on duty at the bakery store, she came in all a glow and bubbling over and said that she had just come back from the show "Red Shoes," and it was simply a marvelous production. Believe me, I didn't know anything about that show then, and I know very little about it now. There was a lady in the store at the same time, and she was very pleasantly surprised that a person so young could find "Red Shoes" so interesting and entertaining. To my limited knowledge, I think it deals with ballet. In the line of entertainment, she also found "The Sound Of Music" to her liking and to the extreme. As a matter of fact, we saw it several times. I found it to be a very good production too, but I am not prone to seeing it over and over, but I was accommodating.

I have searched my mind for every bit of information I could write on the history of your mother. Keep in mind that all of this happened before we were married. Now, as time surely will go on, we approached the vital moment of making our plans of marriage into reality.

One evening we were at Lola's house. She lived on 71st Street now since her father bought a home for $7,500. The home is on seventy-first and very close to the street named Park Avenue. The home is a light brown shingled home located next to a store that had a butcher shop. Right across the street is a delicatessen store owned by a man named Arango.

I have very happy memories of going to that store with my grandfather. My sister, Marilyn, and I would sleepover at our grandparents' house, and for a treat, my grandfather would take us across the street and buy us a bag of chips and a pop. Since we didn't have pop and chips too often, it was really special. Or it could be that it was really special because it was time spent with my grandparents.

This particular evening, I mentioned that we should talk seriously about setting a date for our marriage. She responded that this was not likely since I did not even ask her to marry me. I said, "What do you suppose I am doing now?" she answered that it sounded more like a discussion of a wedding and not a proposal. So, my retort was, "What do you want me to do, get on one knee and ask you to marry me?". She shocked me when she said "YES" and was very serious about it. So I did. That's the way our marriage had its' beginning. Sometime later, I recall being over her home in November on or near Thanksgiving. It started to snow and snow and snow, and then snow some more. By the time I was ready to go home, there were two feet of snow on the ground. I couldn't get my car out of the yard, and it was virtually impossible to walk home in that stuff. She said, "stay overnight," so I did. The next day, going right past Lola's home, was a bride, all in white, walking to Sacred Heart Church! This gal really wanted to get married. I had to add that since I was very impressed.

We began to plan our wedding now in earnest. The date was set for August 18, 1951. Sol Sherwin, my good friend, baked the cake and catered the whole affair. We were married in Immaculate Heart of Mary Church and held the reception at the Polish People's Home or Hall on 71st Street near Fleet, or in between Fleet and Lancing. It was a very nice affair, and Lola made a very radiant bride. That night we had the bridal suite at the Westlake Hotel, and the following morning, we drove out to Mackinac Island to spend our honeymoon.

Just to keep the record straight, we didn't drive all the way out in one day. We spent the night in a hotel in Lansing, Michigan. For that occasion, I had brought along a magnum of champagne. This was to no avail, however, since Lola "had a case of seriously mixed emotions brought on by the newness of the occasion, homesickness and a sincere love for me. Due to this, she felt guilty that she let me down and tried to apologize for her feelings. Yet, I told her this was not necessary. I understood, and we would have many days in the future. She understood and felt better about it then. She reminded me of a frightened little bunny at that moment. The next day we were on our way to Mackinac Island. When we arrived in Mackinac City, we discovered that there had been a mix-up in our reservations. They had a room for us in the city but not on the Island. It worked out, though, since they made contact with the Island and got us a room. But, what a room! The room had twin beds that squeaked and no bathroom. To go to the bathroom, we had to go down to the end of the hall. It was pathetically funny, and we laughed about it, and the honeymoon on the Island was fantastic, simply because we were together. We took bike rides, carriage rides, hikes, shopped, and went sightseeing. But most importantly, we enjoyed each other. I want to mention that your mother was still tense in certain areas in our new relationship and kept her virginity all the way home. This, I regard, as a very fine tribute to her since this was a reflection of her honesty and purity. She was always willing, but it took time to become accustomed to her new role as a wife.

We set up housekeeping at her mother and fathers' home, but from the beginning, I could see that this is not exactly what she wanted. There always seemed to be a bit of conflict between her and her mother, not a flagrant conflict, but more in a subtle vein. Your mother knew where her priorities were, and the first time her mother brought me into the conversation to be criticized, Lola told her in very simple and emphatic language, "That is my husband you are talking about, and I won't ever stand for it. Say one more word, and I am leaving!" This set the tone for months to come and made living there more or less comfortable. There were conflicts, of course, with her mother because her mother did have a rather explosive nature in her younger years. Yet, she cannot be held entirely responsible for this since Walter Fedor was the type of person who at times exhibited behavior that provoked explosiveness. By and large, though, they lived out their lives together perhaps as well as they could. This eventually grew to be old hat to Lola, and we started to look for a place to rent. We found a rental on Rathbone Avenue, and we moved in with baby Susan. Marilyn had not been born yet.

We lived there for a few years, and it was a nice place, and we were happy there together. There was one thing wrong, though, since there were no cold air returns. It was cold in the rooms in the winter, especially on very cold days. It would be common to find snow on the windowsills. Inside the house, I would wear an overcoat watching TV in the living room. Fortunately, the kitchen and baby's room weren't too bad, so we managed. During that period of our married life, Marilyn was conceived, and when Lola's labor pains came very close, I drove her to Grace Hospital on a cold early January morning. Now we had two little babies on Rathbone Avenue. Incidentally, that night as I was getting ready to drive Lola to the hospital, Susan stood up in her crib, red flannel pajamas and all, and said in her best English, "Me go too!!". She did, right over to grandma's house. Your grandmother loved both of you dearly and fussed over both of you as only a real grandmother can. Your grandfather, too, was tickled pink with both of you, and there was no love lacking there either.

The length of time we lived on Rathbone escapes me. However, the way it came about that we moved doesn't. During this time, you two were being supported by my earnings from the bakery I owned with my brother John. My father worked with us, and he really was the boss of the operation even though we were the owners. On occasions, your mother would come to the bakery either on a Saturday or Sunday so we could spend some time together since the bakery demanded much of my time. Lola would take care of the store on Saturday while I did some repair work on the premises. I must emphasize that this was not standard practice since I wanted neither side of either family to get involved in the business to avoid complications. (That is, either John's wife or mine.) It wasn't a family affair, just a simple partnership with my brother. At times it wasn't really that simple.

One Sunday afternoon, when Lola and I left the bakery on our way home, we happened to drive down East 53rd Street. We passed the house that we presently live at and the house that you and Marilyn were raised in. Lola saw the "For Sale" sign in the window and said, "Let's go back and see what that house looks like inside." We did. The house appealed to her, and she said, let's buy it. So, we told the owners that we were interested and asked them how much they wanted. The asking price was $13,000 or in that range. That put it out of our price range since, at that time, 1/3 down was required, and we only had $3,500 in cash. We told the seller that we wanted to buy but that our down payment was too small, but if they changed their price in the future to meet our down payment, we would buy the house. Six weeks later, they called and said they dropped the asking price of the house to $11,500. We made the deal and moved in shortly thereafter.

At that time, there was no cement drive, no overhead garage doors, and no aluminum siding. The house also had a coal furnace. We made all these improvements as we went and made a home for the four of us. For three solid years, everything was just perfect. However, this didn't come about accidentally since Lola, and I had to make a slight correction in our approach to one another. It seemed that I was becoming less communicative and unreasonable as time went on, and this eventually culminated in a confrontation that set our marriage on its' correct course. One day Lola exploded at me and said, "What is happening to you? We can't seem to talk together about anything anymore!". It was then that we sat at the kitchen table and had a long talk. We agreed to listen to each other and consider what each of us said to each other. We agreed to consider each other's ideas and feelings truthfully and respectfully. From then on we got along fine, not always arguing, but always knowing that we were a team working toward the same better goal.

Lola kept the house well and was strong-willed enough to get what she wanted. For instance, she kept mentioning a round braided rug she would like to have for the dining room. After mentioning it several times and getting the same response, "We can't afford it right now." I came home one day and found the carpet on the floor to my shocking surprise. My stupid remark "What's this doing here?" simply evoked the response, "It's the carpet I wanted, and we can afford it in payments." So that was that since there really wasn't anything else to say. Of course, I smiled to myself secretly and admired her spunk, for it was a worthwhile addition to the home. Yes, we did pay it off, and very easily.

However, the biggest caper she pulled (and she proved a little larceny in her heart by this) yet this again was for something she really wanted. We had made an agreement to purchase only things by cash and not get overloaded by charges since we had a $6,500 mortgage to pay off. Yet, secretly, she started to buy a "dinner wear set, piece by piece, week by week, and put it away, I presume until she had the whole set. There was a fly in the ointment, however, since I happened to be at home one day unexpectedly when a china piece was delivered. That's when it hit the fan. But of course, the die was cast, and she completed the whole set. My objection to this was that she could have bought the whole set in a regular store for half the amount. The Melmac was good, though, and there are still plates here that are being used. You no doubt get the impression that your mother had a tenacious and persistent manner to insist on things important to her, but it was never in an overbearing or obnoxious manner. Her tact was steady and disarming but always tempered with a sweet personality.

Back to the chapter on the Melmac Caper. You have read about a method your mother used to get something she really wanted. This called to mind another incident involving a refrigerator. We went to a so-called "wholesale place" to buy a refrigerator. After looking over all of the refrigerators in the place, she kept coming back to an Admiral that caught her eye. Now while we were shopping, I tried to steer her into buying a GE. The GE products have always been dependable, and I know from experience that my mother had a GE that ran and ran and never broke down. She really wanted the Admiral, though, so I bought it. The box lasted about two years, then would suddenly get hot. When you pulled the plug and let it rest, it would cool again and run for a while. Then it would turn hot inside again. I got rid of that box and bought a Hotpoint, which is a GE. It is still in the kitchen and running to this day.

In these past summaries of past events, you may get the impression that I was a soft touch and yielded to Lola's every wish. This really is not so since we did discuss all issues democratically. The point is this; I was always of the opinion that the homemaker spends a lot more time in the home than the man. Since this is the case, she sees the furnishings more often than the man. If she really hates a piece of furniture or an appliance that is not to her liking, she has to look at it all day long, day in and day out. This, no doubt, would get to her in time and could reflect in her outlook in life and could directly reflect back to me. So, why rock the boat?

Time has taken its' toll in its' healing action and has dulled my memory of many events that transpired in our lives. Those that I have mentioned were of a "lasting impression and sufficient to give you a better concept of your mother's personality, nature, and idiosyncrasies. Since you did request it, Susan, I decided to write it out for you and Marilyn so that on occasions, if you wish, you could read it again from time to time. When I think back to my mother and father, I would wish they could have written something like this for me.

In the proceeding pages, I mentioned that everything ran smoothly and perfectly for us for the first three years. But one evening, Lola had just gotten back from church. There was some sort of doing there. She said she felt funny and wondered out loud as to what was happening to her. This was the beginning of the downhill slide in her health. From then on, it was hospital after hospital. This lasted about 13 years.

I am not about to give a detailed account of those thirteen years, but I will just touch generally on some of the facts that should be known. Some of these facts certainly enhanced our faith and brought us closer to our God.

If this lasted 13 years, and my mom died at 36, I would say she was about 23 or 24 when she felt this way. It must have been 1954 or 1955. I

was born in 1952 when my mother was 21 years old. My sister was born in 1955 when my mother was almost 24 years old. Pregnancy takes a toll on someone with Lupus, so I would think that my mom probably started feeling sick after the birth of my sister. At the time, she did not know that she had Lupus.

There too, was its' share of many anxious moments, frustrations, anticipations, let-downs, and tears. Throughout those trying years, however, we had more than most people achieve in a lifetime (or perhaps never do). We had each other as husband and wife and as friend to friend, but more deeply. Our spirits were in tune with each other in this fight for survival. The same spirit of Christ that dwells in all of us welled up in both of us and gave us a true unity. All the silly frills of life were stripped away, and life was exposed in all its rawness. Yet, we saw the real importance of our existence, knew where we came from, and knew who to trust and seek out for help. The help came in deeper spiritual trust. The outcome in human terms would be called a failure. Yet the things I observed through the course of your mother's suffering would give her the status of "Heroic." Since she carried her cross rather silently, even when, at times, I knew she suffered deep emotional and physical pain.

My mother did suffer physical and emotional pain. I remember seeing her with a walker at times, slowly walking up to the communion rail at church to receive the blessed sacrament, and of course, there was that peaceful smile. Somehow her positive attitude and faith in God kept her going even with her physical and emotional trials.

One Sunday, there was a bake sale at our church. Since my dad was still a baker at that time, my mom asked me to walk the two blocks to our church and drop off some bakery items my dad had brought home to donate to the sale. My mom could not go herself as she did not feel well that day. She was still in bed. My dad was working because as a baker, he worked seven days a week. I got ready; went to my mother's bedroom door to tell her I was leaving. When I called her, she did not answer. I turned on the light and saw my mother shaking and twisting in the bed. At the time, I did not know what was happening. Now I know that she was having a convulsion. I had to call the operator because 911 was not in existence yet and ask her to send an ambulance. By the time they got to our house, the convulsion was over, and my mom got up to go to the bathroom. She was confused and did not feel well.

Even so, she made sure that the men that came to help her did not see her going to the bathroom. I remember her asking me to shut the door so she could have some privacy. After that, they took her to the hospital in the ambulance. I went with her because my dad did not make it home from work in time. While we were waiting in the emergency room, my mom said to me, "Something is happening!" She then proceeded to have another convulsion. Because of the possibility that she could have a convulsion at any time, my parents kept a bundle of popsicle sticks taped together on their bedpost. When my mom would have a convulsion, my dad would have to put these sticks between her teeth to prevent her from biting her tongue. If she bit it hard enough or enough times, the blood or tissue could have gotten stuck in her throat and caused her to choke. I don't think this is recommended any longer, but at the time, it was common practice. My mom's convulsions were caused by the poisons that would accumulate in her blood; her kidneys could not filter them out as they were supposed to do. She was literally filled with toxins that could not be eliminated from her body.

Together we found untapped strength that we were not aware we had, and each day was very meaningful. I also recall that your mother had a deep spiritual commitment. For example, she belonged to the Franciscan Order Third Oder of St. Francis and attended an afternoon meeting and mass once a month at a church on 30th Street. It is St Joseph by name. This church embraces the Franciscan tradition. They met in quiet prayer and had a meeting afterward. I must admit that your mother asked me to go to an "occasionally" meeting, and I did reluctantly. It wasn't that I'm adverse to St. Francis since my name is the same as his, and I honor him as a great saint, but I hadn't learned that type of subdued service then. Today, there is another "Francis" in the recently deceased Padre Pio, whose original name was Francis but changed it to Pio when he became a Friar in the Terterian Order. With your mother was a Franciscan, and Padre Pio a soon-to-be saint (I feel that he is my patron saint already), and my name being Francis, I have a deep affinity now to St. Francis and his order.

Your mother requested that she be buried as a member of the Franciscan order, and she was. She was clothed in a dark chocolate brown, the color of the order, and a white cincture (or rope) with the slippers to match. I'm sure her spirit rested in this attire and declared her spirituality to the very last step of life.

I remember some of these years of my mothers' suffering. Still, as a young child, adolescent, and teenager, I didn't really understand or realize the devastation that was going on in my family. I knew my mother was sick, and she spent many weeks and sometimes months in the hospital, but since my parents protected me from the real seriousness of the situation, I never really knew that my mom was dying.

Of course, being immature and going through all of the changes of growing up, I did not appreciate what a blessing it was to have such a wonderful, unique woman for my mother. As an adult, I realize what a tremendous loss it is not to have her in my life, not only for myself but also for my children, who I know she would have loved dearly.

As a teenager, I gave my parents some heartaches. This was especially true the year she died. As a 14-year-old, not quite 15, I was going through a rebellious stage. Of course, there was a boy involved. He was arrogant and was not very respectful. To me, he was wonderful. Obviously, my parents did not approve. They wanted me to break up with him. I was not allowed to date until I was 16 years old, so we did not go out, but I would meet him around the neighborhood, and we would hang out.

I was so much in puppy love with this boy that he and I even talked about running away and getting married since our parents did not approve and we wanted to be together. I don't know how my parents found out, but they sat me down and had a long talk with me, explaining just what it would be like to be married to this boy. They also pointed out some other things that made me see him in a different light. Good for them and good for me. I eventually did break up with him. I guess he did not want the same thing. He told his mother that I had written him a note telling him that I wanted to resume our relationship. His mother called my mother and told her about this. I had not written the note, and I told my mother so. After all that had gone on, my mother believed me. She told his mother, "My daughter said she did not write

the note, so she did not write it." This may seem like a minor thing, but I never forgot that after everything I put them through, including lies, my mother still trusted me and believed me.

I am attempting to write a true and factual account of the nature and personality of your mother. I am not attempting to create a myth or cause an illusion as to the true nature and attributes of Lola Traska, but I am paying tribute to a fine person whom I recognize as such. Let me emphasize that she was truly human, warm and considerate, compassionate and loving, but she could lose her temper at times and scold if the situation warranted it.

Before I go into other things and forget some of the things that come to mind, I had better write them down so you may know your mother better.

She was developing into a very good cook and took pride in putting out a good meal. In her younger days, she rode a bike, played tennis, and swam. Her swimming was much better than ordinary since, on many occasions, I would see her swim long distances out to the middle of a lake to the diving board and raft located there. The distance involved in that swim was considerable, perhaps 200 feet or so.

In the area of compatibility toward a husband, your mother was uninhibited in giving of herself. She realized that a man and a woman united in marriage became one flesh, and since we are created by God, the body is holy, totally from head to toe, every part of it. Each person in the marriage realizing this, knowing that God made us for each other could enjoy each other fully. This is His gift to each person in marriage; providing their expression of love to each other is also a manifestation of their love for God. We did this always, realizing that the joy we experienced could not have been possible unless God had made it so, and we gave Him thanks and acknowledged Him.

This was not intended to be a theological treatise, but I feel this is relevant to this summary. After all, you don't get to know someone until you know their feelings, ideas, and thoughts. We are all human with emotions, attributes, and defects of character. To be able to really express your feelings to the other person without repercussions is a tribute to the other person involved. This is truly a good way to unlock the hidden repression we all can carry and makes us prisoners from within.

A facet of your mother's personality was her inner understanding. I should like to relate a specific incident that occurred during the days of my drinking that bears out her tolerance, patience, and understanding. While I drank, I cannot recall her nagging me about it at any time. This annoyed me at times, simply because I could never blame her for my drinking. One day, when I ran out of liquor and desperately needed to get out for a drink, I tried my best to provoke her into an argument so that I could storm out of the house for a drink (or two or ten), but she would not go for it. So, I just left anyway. I returned after several hours, her attitude had not changed, and she was just as sweet and tolerant as ever. This was good because there could have been a real serious situation develop at that point. To lend an air of realism to this past episode, I suspect that my future AA sponsor's wife had filled her in on how to deal with alcoholism.

A related incident occurred sometime later, and after I had been admitting to myself that my drinking was not normal. I specify "to myself" since I would not admit this to anyone else. When the day came that I admitted it to her, and I did it with great emphasis that "I felt trapped within myself, as if in prison, and felt like a prisoner", she said to me very matter-of-factly, "When you really decide you had enough, you will stop." She said this so sincerely without malice or anger that I was profoundly impressed. There are words I carried with me for years deep in my heart. This made me realize that she saw a strength in me that I didn't know was there. This was very helpful later getting and staying sober. She also said to me, "If I should die, don't get drunk because of me!" This also stuck with me and helped me greatly because I didn't get drunk when she died. She was clever enough to let me know that I couldn't blame her if I got drunk, but also that she wanted her love to extend beyond the grave and wished me well always.

Another incident that I call to mind is the cherry tree. This brought out her inner strength and demonstrated her ability to be insistently forceful without being obnoxious. I told her that the cherry tree was dying and that I was going to cut it down. She asked if it was possible to save the tree, and I said, "Yes, I think so." In her own sweet way, yet you could detect a very definite veiled command in her request she said, "Don't cut it down, save the tree!"

Needless to say, the tree is still standing in the backyard. The tree is getting sick, though, and I don't know if I can save it now, but I am reminded that that tree lives because of her, and I wouldn't dare cut it down unless it were completely dead. Also, because of her insistence, there have been many cherry pies that we have enjoyed.

There too, was the usual concern for her children and the love that she manifested in her words and actions. She would scrub you up, primp you up, and exhibited the right number of hugs and kisses that a loving mother would. Then there were the times that she would pop you both in the car (a red rambler station wagon) and go shooting off with the radio blasting, laughing, and having fun in your company.

I sure do remember these car outings. My mother would slowly but surely turn up the radio volume, laughing each time she did it until the music was full blast. After laughing about this silliness together, we would turn it down to a tolerable volume, and then we would sing along. There were also trips to Higbee's downtown. She would dress us up, and we would go to the Silver Grill for lunch. I remember the menus that were in the shape of a little stove and the goldfish swimming in a concrete pond as you entered the restaurant. It was a special time that my mom, my sister, and I spent together. I know my mom loved us very much and was proud of us. She loved being a mom to us, and she loved for us to be together and have a good time.

We as a family were "loose as a goose," you might say in spite of the illness that beset us. There were the light moments that were, of course, generated by the relaxed attitude we both developed through confidence in each other due to trust and an earned compatibility.

"One day, I decided to really blow her cork by pulling a gag on her that would make any homemaker FLIP. Years ago, there was a place downtown called Gene's Fun House. I went there and bought a sort of attachment that you plug into a cigarette that was rather short. The attachment had wire at one end that fits into the butt of the cigarette. On the other end, the wire was connected to simulated cigarette ash that looked positively real. This incidentally had to be at least an inch and a quarter long—something like this.

Then my father drew a picture of it.

Well, I waited until Lola was cooking a big pot of soup. When she was out of the room, I put this fake ash onto the butt of my cigarette, bent the ash as if it were ready to fall off. I put my head very close to the surface of the soup with the ash hanging precariously from the butt and called her over under the pretense of asking something about the soup. You can well imagine her reaction when she walked in and saw me right over the pot with that big ash hanging from my cigarette. As she became aware of the situation and could have a full grasp of it, I kept talking with this fake cigarette and ash in my mouth, and the ash kept bouncing up and down and threatening it would fall in the soup any second. She said, "STOP! Don't move, don't talk, move back!!!" Anyway, you can imagine how you would react to something like this. Yes, we did laugh about this and many other things. We did enjoy each other's company.

Lola was sensitive to other people and their needs and truly cared about them. It was a grasp of the 2nd commandment that staggered my imagination. I couldn't conceive how she could be concerned in such an honest manner. It is difficult to follow this "Love one another, as I have loved you" when you are feeling well, yet she felt that way even when she was desperately ill. I even said to her, "Honey, you have a full grasp of what Christ is telling us, now if you only accept your mother that way, you will have a direct route to heaven."

To clarify, you would have to understand that at this time, her mother had become a very heavy burden to her. At one time, Emily had at least eight different doctors she was going to at the same time, and it became a drag to both of us. It is understandable why she was difficult to accept. Be aware, too, that all of this was happening during Lola's illness, and she is the one who needed to be attended to instead of her mother. Yet, Lola tried to do the best she could but was annoyed at times.

Lola and her mother got along fairly well or perhaps very well throughout their lives, but it is important to remember that an only child could have been subjected to a little more possessiveness than in a family of more than one. Lola was the apple of her father's eye and could manipulate him if this was her inclination. This does not suggest that she took advantage of him excessively, but on occasions, it did come out to her best interests. Overall, she was well-balanced and a wonderful person.

I remember that after my grandfather died, my grandmother was very reluctant to live alone. So, she eventually moved in with us. I am

not sure why she needed to go to so many doctors, but I remember feeling or somehow getting the drift that she needed to have attention or a reason to remain living with us. My mother was very ill at the time, and I do remember the toll it took on her. She had gotten to the point where she was having convulsions and was very weak. Finally, my father had to put my grandmother in a nursing home. She agreed to go. I guess her anxiety about living alone even went so far that she was willing to consent to begin living in a nursing home. I believe she was somewhere in her 60's at this time. She lived there until her death in her 90's.

"Your mother had been hospitalized many times."

I remember my mother being in the hospital many times and for long periods. One time, in particular, I remember visiting her in the hospital on Christmas Day. I remember her asking me what Santa had brought me. I told her that I got a bride doll. She asked me questions about it, what it was wearing, what it looked like, did it have a wedding ring. When I told her the doll did not have a wedding ring, she seemed very disappointed. She asked me if I was sure there wasn't a ring. As a little girl, I didn't understand why this would bother her so much. To this day, I am not sure if the doll was supposed to come with a ring. My mom perhaps felt helpless because she could not do anything about it since she was in the hospital. Or if maybe she just felt sad because she was not at home on Christmas day to enjoy her daughters opening their gifts from Santa Claus. When I think of that now, I realize that somehow, she did make sure that my sister and I had gifts from Santa under the tree even though she was in the hospital trying to get well. She truly loved us and wanted us to have as normal a childhood as was possible even though she was sick.

I will list the hospitals that she was in, and some of them were more than once. She was at Marymount Hospital initially, where their initial diagnosis was nephritis, which is a pesky disease but certainly not fatal and could be controlled. Later, Lola went to St. Alexis at least twice. She went to Cleveland Clinic several times. One stay was 118 days in length. The first visit was an emergency. Your mother was full of water and poisons and went on a dialysis machine. It corrected her chemical imbalance and removed the poisons from her system. She responded well to this treatment, and without it, would have died at that time. In this same vein, the man who invented the dialysis machine was Doctor Kolf, and it was my pleasure to meet this man and thank him personally. He was at the Cleveland Clinic at the time, and by chance, I saw him in the hallway and asked him if I could speak to him. I was very disturbed about your mother's condition and just needed to talk.

Men of this caliber are usually preoccupied with other thoughts. This remarkable man stopped in his tracks, gave me a moment of his time, answered all of my questions, and exhibited true compassion that left a lasting impression. He said, "take all the time you want," and acted in a genuinely caring manner. I don't know why all great men dress like farmers who just pull out the suit to go into town occasionally, but that is the way he looked. Unpretentious and with kindness that reflected from his eyes and all of his person. After talking to him, I thanked him for inventing the dialysis machine. He answered humbly and said, "I wish it worked better than it does." This man is certainly in the history books with Pasteur, Edison, etc. Most importantly, he is a great person internally.

During an illness as tragic as your mother's, there are many instances where God will manifest Himself in the inner working of the fabric of the ensuing drama of life, reminding us that we are not alone in our dastardly predicament. On one such occasion, when your mother had just been admitted to Mt. Sinia Hospital and put in a room on the second floor, she was distraught over the fact that she would need regular blood transfusions. The transfusions were secondary in her mind; it wasn't the discomfort she dreaded; it was because she had received so much blood in the past. I had managed to get blood from the police department and a factory blood bank at Tapco. So much in fact that we felt we had worn out our welcome, had come to a brick wall, had no money, and had run out the string. I assured her in good faith that the good Lord was aware of the situation. He would not let us down and was right there in the room, right now, hearing this conversation. After all, she had been through; I could understand her dismay and depression. Yet, it is a fact that God is aware of us in life because He is life.

I left shortly after and was walking in the main corridor of the hospital heading outdoors when a man hooked me by the arm and said, "I hear you need a lot of blood!!" He explained that he was the assistant director and that there were eleven blood cards about to expire. He said he would put them all on my account, and Lola would be all set for the next eleven months. Of course, I couldn't thank him enough, but I made a fast beeline back to your mother with the news. This was good for her faith, and we drew strength from this in the Lord.

Another incident that is worth mentioning, and fixed in my memory, happened one rainy, windy, stormy night. Since your mother's illness was constantly on my mind and I always felt that there must be a solution somewhere, I always had hope and always searched. It was dark that night with the rain coming down in torrents. There was a wind that came in waves, and in it was a miserable night to be out. I was driving in my car on Fleet Avenue, not far from Seventy-First Street, and was driving toward 65th and home. It was then that I spotted a dark figure fighting its way against the wind and pouring rain. I stopped the car and offered a ride to this unknown person, and he accepted with great relief. As he entered the car, I learned that he was a missionary. He had spent much of his life in foreign countries and was here on leave. I asked him where he was going, and he answered that he was staying at St. Alexis Hospital and had a room there located directly over the boiler room. He said it was hot and noisy there and inferred that they could have done better than that. I mention this because the man impressed upon me that he was a good man and very human.

Through our conversation, it was only natural for me to mention your mother and her condition. He seemed to understand with compassion that had a special comforting, soothing effect. He also said that he had encountered similar conditions and other illnesses as well. In this case, however, he said the people in foreign lands had been helped by a certain blend of tea, that when consumed, flushed the kidneys. I was delighted to hear that he had brought some of this tea back home with him, but he was disappointed that the quantity he could give me was less than he would like. He said he would pray for your mother as well. By this time, we had arrived at St. Alexis, and I drove toward the back of the hospital, past the emergency room. He went up and brought me the tea, giving it to me with his blessing and prayers, mentioning one certain berry in this blend, which he thought was the prime active ingredient. (Incidentally, I identified that berry later as the juniper berry, and it indeed is a diuretic.)

There was no time wasted, your mother and I cooked up this brew, and amazingly it worked fine for a long time. How long, I don't know, but long enough to help buy some time. We ran out of this tea, but by then, I had identified the berry and had read up about it. Juniper berry had been used a long time as a diuretic, and an English doctor tried brewing large quantities of juniper berry tea and putting it in bottles. To assure that the tea wouldn't spoil, he added alcohol to it. The English found it pleasant to drink and adopted it as a beverage, and thus – Gin was invented. I found a huge supply of the berry at Gus Galucci's downtown, near where the old downtown market had been.

Throughout your mother's illness, I tried everything possible to be of help. An article once in Prevention Magazine dealt with edema and bananas' beneficial effects in relief of this condition. It suggested going on a strictly banana diet for several days. It went on to explain that since the banana had potassium, other minerals and contained pectin (an ingredient easy on the stomach), it could be helpful to the body. At this time, Lola's blood pressure was very high, and her body was full of water. It had filled all of her body, had entered one of her breasts to the point that it had expanded to a much larger proportion than the other. Lola and I were in agreement that we should search all areas of possibilities for help. I told her about the banana diet, and she said: "Let's try it."

I bought a whole case of bananas from a small fruit store that was located on East 71st Street, not too far from Harvard Avenue. We started on the diet immediately. There were favorable results in a few days, the water did pass, and a dramatic drop in Lola's blood pressure occurred. It was touch and go for many years; the eroding effects of her illness could only be deterred by Juniper berries and bananas, etc., but she could not be arrested. Thank God that today, almost twenty or more years later, there have been dramatic advances in the treatment of this disease, and more effective medicines have been discovered for treatment. I know a few people today with this illness are leading normal lives. Thank God!!!

Your mother's illness lasted a number of years, perhaps ten or so, until her death on September 18, 1967. The events before her death stand out in my mind since it was a Sunday, and we went to church and after to the social hall for some type of gathering. She was in a good mood and seemed to enjoy herself. In the crowd, I lost her for a few minutes, but when I found her, she told me she had had a small glass of wine in a toast to someone or something. I did mention that this may not have been a good idea since her kidneys did not filter at all, and alcohol was a poison chemically. Later in the afternoon, she went to a shower at home on East 54th Street.

When I picked your mother up from the shower, she said that she had an upset stomach, so I gave her some antacid. This was early evening now. Perhaps 5:30 or 6:00 o'clock. I sat with her as she laid on the couch in the living room. The couch was right along the front windows as it generally is. This, however, is just an added detail with perhaps very little significance, except for the fact that when I did see your mother that Monday morning, I glanced from the dining room and realized that there was something drastically wrong.

To backtrack, we sat together, and I did what I could for her, even mentioning that I would skip my Sunday AA meeting so I could attend to her needs. Yet she insisted that she would be alright and that I should go to the meeting. So I did. When I returned, her condition was about the same, with the upset stomach reoccurring occasionally, but she also had his odd, hollow cough, which I later learned develops when the heart is failing.

I remember lying in my bed upstairs and hearing my mother cough. She coughed pretty frequently, but at the time, age 15, I had no idea that my mother would die that night.

We sat together until about midnight when she suggested that I should lie down on the bed in the bedroom off of the dining room and rest. Well, she must have insisted, because I did, mentioning that if she needed me for anything she should, just call. That was the last time I saw her alive; I found her lying on the couch that Monday morning, lying on her back with her left knee in a raised position. The moment I glanced over from the dining room, I said, "Oh my God!" My worst fears were verified when I walked over and tried to awaken her. I will not embark on a play-by-play of the rest of the day because it is not necessary, but it was a long, empty day. I do recall that I went upstairs in the hallway and at the end of the hall was a picture of Jesus. I knelt in front of the picture and asked Him for His strength to get me through these times. Jesus did not disappoint me; I stayed sober through all of this and have been ever since.

It wasn't that I didn't plan on getting drunk that evening because I bought three bottles of top-grade booze. It was late in the evening when finally, my two sisters left. I was in the living room, sitting in the dark by myself. They had bid me goodnight, and as soon as they left, I went into the kitchen with the intention of taking a few drinks. As I entered the room, a very strong thought in the form of a question overwhelmed me and said or asked, "Did you love her?" It was so real that I answered out loud, "YES!" Then a second strong thought came through, saying, "If you really loved her, how will you look tomorrow in the funeral parlor staggering around drunk?" This was enough for me, and I have been sober ever since.

When I think back, I have to wonder if my mother knew she would die soon. About a week before her death, she did not feel well. She asked me to call one of our neighbors who would be hosting some kind of get-together that my mother was invited to about 4-5 days in the future. She wanted to tell them that she could not attend because she wasn't feeling well. I hesitated and said, "Mom, why don't we wait to call. You might feel better by then." However, she was adamant that I call that day. She wanted them to have enough notice so that they knew how to plan for the event. So I made the call.

My memory has just about been exploited to the fullest; time has dimmed much of the pain and sharpness of the details. Yet every person is shaped by the events of his or her life, good experience or bad, in some way or another. So it is with me, perhaps a little more compassionate, a little more faithful, a little wiser, a bit more understanding. Through a humbling experience such as this, it appears that God first hollows us out so there will be room for better things, better gifts. When I reflect on this suffering, which seems so meaningless and cruel, it does have its rewards as the Hand of God shapes the clay vessel. I should stop in mid-course of life at times and ask, "Will I benefit, or will I accept the resulting gift of God from these tribulations, or will I reject them?" It is not my intention to drift off into a full theological dissertation in these writings. Still, I intend to inject a few of my thoughts and share just a few of my personal experiences that may benefit you if you wish to gain a little better knowledge of me.

It has been said that we are three distinct characters. One the person we think we are. Two the person others think we are, and the three the person we are. In all of the experiences that your mother and I lived through, she said to me, "You are Job." This, to me, is the ultimate compliment. Please understand that this is what she saw and what she thought, and what she felt. It in no way should infer that I am suggesting a pat on the back for me. However, it should emphasize that I not only tried to be a husband but also a friend. My definition of a friend may vary widely with others' concepts of what a friend is. For me, a friend is a rare bird indeed. The Lord Jesus Himself, throughout His teachings, keeps instructing us on friendship. I feel that all people have this urge for friendship, but our humanity gets in the way for all of us.

Here again, I do not wish to get into all of the defects of character that we all possess, but it is important to stress that they do mute the quality of life we live and rob us of the full life intended for us. As surely as God has said, "Seek and you will find," which indicated to me, His revelation of Himself in His creation and in His word. As God stated, "Come, and I will show you." He intends to reveal more and more of Himself to us, but only to those who are sincere of heart. Peter's brother, Andrew, asked Jesus, "Where do you live?" Jesus said, "Come, I will show you!" Andrew was so impressed by that short visit that he brought Peter to Christ the next day. You know the rest of the story of St. Peter, I am sure. God approaches us in all positive aspects and wants us to believe in Him and come to Him.

This is the 17th of January 1985. It is my 66th birthday. This summary is drawing to a close, and I need to mention just two or three more incidents or happenings that seem relevant to these writings. This first account, there is no basis of proof I can offer except for the fact that it has remained in my memory for many years. It happened a short time after your mother's death one evening. As I sat in the living room and all the lights were out. It was dark in the room, and I dwelt upon all of the things that had happened. Either I was asleep or in a "twilight doze" or whatever. But in this particular state, I saw myself being enlightened by your mother. The message was this "Frank, as I lay on the couch, I felt a gentle tugging away from my body. I rose above it and saw myself lying there, then I looked over into the corner of the room and saw two men standing there with their arms outstretched, indicating that I should go with them.

There were two or three moments in that period that I went into some kind of meditation or whatever it was, trying to get a more detailed input that never came. My efforts apparently did not go unrewarded, however. I got no verbal message, but I did get, as if out of the blue, a strong perfume scent that was intense and extremely pleasing. This happened about three times on separate occasions. My sense of smell has never been that good, yet I smelled this. I cannot identify the scent, but I would guess that violets probably smell like that, yet I don't know what violets smell like. Figure that out if you can. Oh yes, I did check for the source of it. Aftershave, something spilled, etc. Yet, there was no logical explanation for it. However, the incident gave me a better feeling about everything on each separate occasion that it happened.

It wasn't until years later that I had another experience with the scent of perfume on my way home from Aunt Carrie's in Solon. You may be interested in this experience too, so I shall relate the events of that particular day. I had been to Solon visiting my sister Carrie. It was the winter season, yet I can't say specifically what month it was. The day was overcast, rather cold with all the bleakness of the sleeping trees, dead weeds, and leaves along the roadside as I drove home. Route 43 was sparsely settled with perhaps a house here or there. As I drove along, my car, the maroon 1969 – 88 olds, was suddenly full of the scent of roses. The scent was heavy but not to the point of being obnoxious. It was pleasant and surprising and aroused my curiosity as to the origin. The scent lasted perhaps 30 seconds to a minute, which really should be of no consequence at all, but what is important is that the scent happened suddenly and disappeared suddenly with no lingering trace at all.

This caused me to wonder about the significance of this occurrence since this is not a commonplace everyday thing. For years I could not correlate any attachment to this event, but it impressed itself on my mind. Years later, at an AA meeting, my friend Bob and I were recounting unusual events that had happened in our lives. The rose scent incident came up in the conversation, and Bob said quite casually, "Oh, you had a visit from Padre Pio." I asked him to explain since the name was unfamiliar to me. He answered that Padre Pio was a monk in Italy who had the unusual power of Bi-location. He could be in two places at the same time in any part of the world, the distance being no obstacle. He could either show himself in a body or make his presence known by the scent of violets or roses. Bob brought me a book about him, since then I have read all literature I could find about this saintly man. He has become a part of my life and has made a difference in me.

There are many things I could write about in our interactions, but perhaps again in some future letters as I should like for both of you to know a little about me too. Maybe it could be of interest and passed down to future generations as the beginning of our family tree. I am sure that I would have liked to read about descendants of my past and their history of make-up and myriads of personalities.

The next event that is of significance happened the day following your mother's funeral. In my emotionally drained condition, I reasoned that it would be important to get back into the mainstream of life. To start doing things that are normal, back to daily activities and develop a system of continuity. Believe me; it was not easy to "bring the body, and the mind will follow." Anytime we suffer an emotional amputation such as this, the mark is there inescapably, and the burden is crushing. Yet, through this, we learn of God's awareness of our situation and opportunity for growth. This does not become apparent for a long time since the burden blinds us with its oppressive weight. Yet, in this case, God made it known that He will not give us more than we can bear. This, too, could be nullified by our willingness to accept or reject, but if we follow the guideline "To accept the things I cannot change and seek God's strength." He does not disappoint.

My father was the custodian for St. John Nepomucene Church on East 50th and Fleet. When my mother met him, he was a baker and owned the bakery shop on East 57th off Fleet Avenue with his brother John. They eventually sold the bakery, and my father became a security guard at Mount Sinai Hospital. This worked out well for a time since my mom was admitted to that hospital a few times. However, my father wanted to be closer to home since my sister and I were still young, and my mom was not well. I know he prayed about this, and he was offered the job at St. John's church. We lived on East 53rd off of Fleet, just a few blocks away. Added to this was that my father could stop in the church and pray any time he needed comfort and encouragement. I know he did this frequently, so this turned out to be the perfect job for him.

I went back to work the day after your mother's funeral. Compounding my situation was that I was still in the grips of the insidious disease of alcoholism and was in the withdrawal phase. To this point, I had been sober about ten months, but the urges had not altogether subsided, and this is miserable by itself. In conjunction with my grief and being generally run-down, put me in a weakened emotional state. As I walked through the churchyard at St. John's, I stopped between the newly built garage and rectory, standing on the sidewalk that runs between them. A week before, I had it all filled in the area with topsoil, leveled and ready to plant grass. There were just a few blades of wild grass sprouting here and there in the mostly barren soil. In my great mental anguish and despair, I bent down and snatched up some grass in my hand, throwing it over my shoulder with reckless abandonment.

At the same time, I said, "Oh my God, why did you allow this?" At that moment, a powerful thought, almost as if it were a voice that said, "Who do you mourn, your wife or yourself?" I turned around; my eyes fell to the sidewalk, the grass I had thrown with such abandonment had formed a perfect green cross on the pavement. I saw life in the green and an invitation to pick up the cross of life. There was a transformation at that moment, a new strength, courage that caused me to go on, for I felt lifted up. Now, as I walked toward the back of school toward my workroom, I swear to this day that I wasn't alone, for I felt two presences accompanying me on each side, offering consolation and encouragement. I swear this to be the truth, for I felt them there, and it felt comforting, warm, and good not to be alone.

The recounts that I have just described, I am sure, could be constructed in many ways. Some would suggest they were caused by great stress. Others would say that emotional instability was a factor. There would be myriads of other explanations and solutions to explain away the causes of the incidents related in the above chapters. If I was the person reading this and someone else had written this and said that they had experienced these things, my skepticism would be a dominant factor. Yet, they happened to me just the way I have written it. I am not too concerned whether anyone accepts or rejects it; I simply had to write it because it did happen as related. As I near the end of this narration, I am about to write about the most amazing thing that has ever happened to me. But before I get into that, another experience that requires mentioning just came across my mind as I begin to write.

You see, I am writing in my basement on an outdoor lounge chair, with a crackling fire in my pot-bellied stove. It is January 20th, 1986, as I draw near the conclusion of these writings. It has been a long time from start to finish, and I feel all those moments have been well spent.

You can be well aware that illness, even in its shortest duration, causes much apprehension, stress, and tension. It is easy to conceive that prolonged illness can cause deep consternation and all its' side effects. You have seen a steady reaching out to God for help, comfort, and strength in my narration. On one occasion, in a deep point of grief and frustration, I came into the basement and picked up an army Bible on my desk. Opening it at random, my eyes fell upon the passage that said in effect, "God has not given you that which is promised for He has something better in store for you." I'll admit that I did question God and wondered why He ignored the fervor of my prayers. Now here I see this passage. Of course, I felt that the page opened to that passage just by chance.

So, I closed the book and tried it again. Same passage again. Well, I said the binding must have gotten stuck in the section, and it opens to that particular page. By this time, I was upstairs in my bedroom. I decided to try it one more time. Same Passage! Well, Thomas had better faith than that, and I felt uplifted by this. The next day, I tried it again, but the page wouldn't open on that passage. I started to search through the book in seriousness for the passage but to no avail. Even today, I have the same Bible, and I have tried the random opening, but it didn't open to that page.

Each day I have resolved to read some of the Bible, this was the resolution I made at the start of this year. Today is February 3rd, 1986. Reading the passages has been enriching since this book is a composite of all of Jesus's teachings. I find Him to be total truth, total love, total intelligence: complete and lacking in nothing. He has become personal to me, and I love everything I learn about Him. So, I must love Him, but I realize that it must be by my actions and not lip service. Just being human, however, can be a detriment since so many times, I stand in the way of myself and block the way. I persist and try again.

In the previous chapters, I alluded to a great event that happened in my life, the greatest event ever. There has been nothing before or after, since then, to even be in the same category. It may be that I told you about his in the past, yet since I have been doing this writing, I have been cajoled many times to put it down on paper. I resisted over and over since I didn't know how to write it effectively or how to describe it with the proper credit due. I feel that I couldn't be presumptuous in assuming just what it was or its cause since I am not too familiar with the supernatural or deep spiritual things. Yet, I do remember this as if it were yesterday. It just leaves good feelings to reflect on it. Keep in mind that this happened well over thirty years ago, but let's get on with it.

"At the beginning of my army days, I was given a small bible by the president, Franklyn D. Roosevelt, as were all the soldiers of World War II. Throughout my days in the service, I would read the scriptures and find solace in the word. Whenever I would read the scriptures during my days in the service, the word always made those days go better. Yet I was not ready to subject myself to reading these verses every day because it interfered with what I wanted to do. When I got out of the service, I still would read the word and found that what I had read would remain with me. When an event would occur in my daily life that could be disturbing, I would remember a verse that would fit that situation, and it was comforting. However, through all of this searching was the feeling that there was something lacking--something missing, almost like a rift between me and the actual contact with God that I desired. At this time, I owned my bakery, and a customer came into the store. I came from the back of the building, which was an apartment, into the front of the building, which was the store. The desire or longing had reached a point of hunger to feel God and be aware of His presence. The customer in the store requested a loaf of bread sliced.

As I went into the break room, this thought was on me. As the bread was being sliced, I said with intensity, "Oh God, if I could just feel your power, just once!" At that moment, I felt a soothing, loving warmth start at the center of the top of my head. It started to flow slowly like molten lava of gold. Slowly and deliberately permeating every fiber of my body, filling even the smallest portion with golden glowing warmth. The flow continued all the way down to the bottoms of my feet. At this time, I was in a TOTAL and COMPLETE state of euphoria. There was a feeling of lightness as if I was weightless, and as I walked into the store with the bread, I felt that I was about a foot off the floor. Now, I was totally engulfed from head to toe with

31

this loving warmth; I said, "Wow, if this is what heaven is like. That's for me!" While in this state, all awareness of the world left me; I was in a state of perfect peace. I hesitated to write this for a long time since I didn't know how to do it justice. I didn't want to convey the wrong impressions. Now I feel it is necessary to share this with both of you (my sister Marilyn and me) since this has been in my heart for a long time. How many times I regret saying, "If I could feel your power JUST ONCE." There has been longing for this glowing gold ever since.

To dispel some of the critics who may read this at some time, I will add that I was sober at the time, didn't even drink at that time. I knew about the power of suggestion, am aware of psychosomatic suggestion, know about neurons in my body and their actions. I knew that imagination and other sources of stimuli could explain this phenomenon logically. To this, I will simply say, how could you give a worldly explanation to an experience that was out of this world? My description is inadequate, believe me, but if you took all of the joys of this world in all my life and made a package of them, this package would equal a grain of sand on all of the beaches of the world. All of the grains of sand of all the beaches would just hint at the totality of that beautiful experience. There is nothing more to say.

God Bless you!
Dad, with Love!

This is the end of the writing my dad wrote about my mom.

The following written account is my concerted effort or disconcerted attempt to write a history of my life. Susan has expressed an interest, yet there must be other people who will find this interesting and perhaps meaningful. This auto-biography will require more time. Yet, I reflect on the thought, "what if my parents or grandparents had done this?" An account of their lives would have been of immeasurable interest and no doubt of great help as well. So as I write this, as honestly as I can, I may run the risk of being vulnerable at times, yet, an accurate account is imperative. Before you anticipate any play-by-play of any activities of my life, dismiss the thought. I am only interested in summarizing who I was and who I have become. I regret that I cannot go back deeply into my parents' background since there was a war that disrupted family trees. However, I do remember my mother's father and mother, although very dimly. They lived on a farm just off of Black Road and had perhaps a hundred acres of land. Their trade was farming, raising cows, sheep, geese, and chickens. They also had cows for milk and butter and hogs for their needs and to sell. I presume that they raised a lot of potatoes as their primary crop, since Uncle Walter, their son, raised potatoes. He took over the farm after the death of my Grandfather and Grandmother. I will list my aunts and uncles later to the best of my memory. There isn't much to the list on my father's side.

Frank Trzaska was born on January 17th, 1920, the seventh of ten children, to Sophia Trzaska and Peter Trzaska. My mother's maiden name was Sobecki, and she was the oldest of four girls. Their names in order of age, Nettie, Tillie, and Frances. My mother also had three brothers named in order of age, Leo, John, and Walter.

My birth was on Harvard Avenue at a bakery shop that my father owned. The bakery was located between East 58th Street from the North and East 57th Street from the South. My delivery was by mid-wife, and at that time, you very rarely heard of anyone going to the hospital to have a baby.

My brothers and sisters were in this order, Walter, Tillie, John, Frances, Helen, Carrie, Peter, Mary. Then there was a sister I never knew named Rose who died at perhaps two years of age. She was standing on an iron fence and slipped down, catching her mouth on the iron picket and tore open her mouth; she bled to death. Peter was killed in a street football game on Harvard Avenue, where the streetcar barns used to be. He was buried on his thirteenth birthday. I had just seen him about 2 hours before his death. I was visiting my Aunt Frances on East 58th Street off Harvard Avenue when he stopped in briefly to deliver a newspaper. Later he got involved in this street football game at the Harvard Car Barns. There was a lot of nice grass to play on, but unfortunately, there was an iron catch basin in the area; Pete fell on that and broke his neck. He died a few hours later. I shall refer to this later in my story as I go along.

Incidentally, the name Car Barns was the accepted name for the main terminal for streetcars, which ran on electricity and got their source of power from a long iron stem in the back of the trolley. The stem then ran right up and connected to the main power line that ran above the car about twenty feet up in the air. This stem had a wheel at the end of it and sat right on the power line; it fitted on the thick wire and rolled on it as the car moved. Often, as the car went around a curve, the wheel would jump off the power line, the conductor had to pull on the stem (which was flexible) and pop the wheel back on. So, car bars stand for the main terminal, and cars changed directions there, were repaired there, etc. We used to hop on the back of them when I was a kid and steal rides, which was very dangerous but also thrilling for kids who don't know any better.

Mary, my sister below Pete in age, died at an early age at about four or five. She was a very delightful person who was blonde-haired and whom I loved deeply. I would take her to the movies on Broadway Avenue to a show called New Broadway Theater. One Sunday afternoon, we went to the movies and had a nice time together. I bought her candy, Bit Of Honey, her favorite kind, and she enjoyed herself very much. I would have to guess I was about 12 years old at the time, but age escapes me. Anyway, who thinks of things like that since I didn't know I would be writing anything like this. Mary and I started home after the show and got caught in a rainstorm that was a veritable washout. We were both soaking wet. Now my memory is a little blurred, but it seems that we got soaked going to the show too, and we sat in the show drying out. She was such a gentle, frail person that I worried she would get sick over this. When she did get sick, which could not have been too long after that, I blamed myself and felt very bad about this for a long time. I don't recall if I ever talked to anyone about this, but I carried this within myself for a long time. She developed Polio, which at that time was called infantile paralysis, and died shortly after. Her death was very devastating to me, as was my brother Pete's. I recall crying a lot and feeling bad about both of their deaths.

In a thumbnail sketch of each family member, I'll start with Walter, my oldest brother. I didn't know him well in my youth since the age difference varied so much. He was the typical so-called Bad Boy who ended up in Mansfield Reformatory and had a history of theft. He was a real tough guy who wasn't afraid of anyone. I realize that a lot of his problems were due to alcoholism. Here was a man who I truly learned to love; in the later years of our lives, I found him to be humorous, warm, tender, and loving, with a latent capacity to care from the heart. This is a man that I miss to this day.

He had the capacity to ingrain himself into you with his strong personality. I could write many chapters about him, but space nor time permits.

Tillie was the second oldest, and I didn't know much about her either in my early childhood. As I got to know her later, she didn't endear herself to me. The things I write though should never be construed as a criticism but more so as what I feel. I can only form an opinion if I have a previous idea of what I think a person should be like. I learned that what a person represents sometimes is just what they know and do. I don't have to like what they are doing, but it doesn't mean that I am 100% right. In later years we did have more in common and did socialize occasionally. I shall never forget one big thing she did for me. When Lola was uptight through her illness due to uremic poisoning and the medication, Tillie came and stayed with her until I got back from work. Her visit that day was very impressive and gratifying to me. Later I tried to help her while she was in a nursing home in Ashtabula. Mom and I visited her a couple of times, which seemed to please her. She died in the nursing home.

Frances came after Tillie; the age differential is perhaps 4 ½ years. Whereas I don't recall much home life with her, she has always left a favorable impression on me. Her style of raising her family was a unique experience to behold. She was firm as needed, gentle at the right moment; in all her efforts, you could see caring and love. We spent times together, many good times when I would deliver bakery to her home. Also, when she later moved to Mackinac Island, we went to visit her. When I delivered bakery, it was usually a Friday; it was always a good sale and the last stop on my route. We would have a few drinks together and get involved in a conversation; it was always the same outcome. The phone would ring, Lola on the phone, and the same question, are you coming home today?

Helen, too, was in the age bracket that we could share things. She was the nervous type in her earlier years, but our relationship was decent. I recall that she was an excellent dresser and had pretty legs. But then, what normal guy wouldn't notice that –even on a sister. She has matured into a fine, splendid person, and it is my privilege to call her sister.

Carrie came next. Carrie is an abbreviation of Caroline. She was truly a beautiful woman. I suspect she succumbed to alcoholism in her final years. However, in her prime years, she was a wonderful person inside and out.

There are many pretty women, but she was beautiful. She had an excellent figure, just the right height, and had charm and elegance about herself. Carrie was talented in athletics and set a record for high jump at South High School. Stella Walsh then invited her to come out and try out for the US Olympic team. Carrie declined the offer. When I asked her why she turned down an opportunity of a lifetime, she replied that all of that training would make her look like a guy. Stella Walsh did not by any stretch of the imagination qualify for any type of beauty award. She was, however, an excellent champion runner who was world-known and of Polish ancestry. (A little by-line to this is perhaps in order since it is a story about me and my life. Stella Walsh would train in Rause Park, bounded by 53rd Street and 52nd Street in Newburg Hts. We kids would use all of that back area behind my mother's home to roam and play. Being raised poor and not very mannerly at that time, Stella would practice running, and we would stand off far enough away and shout at her "Boomantana." This name infuriated her, and she would always outrun us and slap us out. We would get far enough away and shout it again and run away. I suppose this was fun.

Peter was my younger brother, and friend, and buddy. He impressed me because he was talented in playing the mouth organ, never had a lesson, and played it right away with no practice whatever. He was also very fast on his feet and could have been perhaps a runner in his day. Yet his was all aborted by his untimely death. This tragic happening was a memorial event of my life and devastated me.

My father, Peter Trzaska, came from Poland when he was seventeen. His departure was prompted by the Russians who were drafting men for the service at that time. Dad was not in favor of this, so he left for the United States. Whereas dad had never had the opportunity for formal education, he had particular wisdom that I learned to tap into in my later years. He was a baker, and wherever he worked, he always ended up being the foreman. In that particular time, all of the immigrants worked and drank; my father was no exception. He drank so much that, at times, he didn't make it to work. Dad talked German, some French, Polish of course, and did well in Bohemian. His English was choppy but sufficient to get along. We will get back to dad; of course, he's interspersed in my life and an integral part.

My mother, Sophia Sobecki, was a real charmer in her early years as a young lady and mother. Her hair was black and sometimes seemed to have an almost blue sheen to it. She was a victim of the times, a farm girl displaced in the city but showing remarkable fortitude for adaption. We all should feel that our mothers are the best, and I did. My mother had the capacity to love, which conquered the many hardships and difficulties we were forced into surviving. At that time, it was a way of life; we were poor but never realized how poor. When you have never been rich, you cannot identify with that. At any rate, my mother will surface throughout my story because without mother, there would be no story. Yet, in any story of a person, the mother is the most essential and influential. She has many facets and carries so many responsibilities that I feel a real, true, dedicated mother has a special place in the bosom of the Lord.

I was born, January 17th, 1920, at the Harvard address I mentioned before. There is a café there now where my dad originally had his bakery. The bakery was located toward the front of this rather long structure, with living quarters in the back. Right in front of the whole building was the retail outlet or store. I remember going into the bakery, and the bakers would give me a piece of dough to play with. I would have been about three years old. Adults made the usual comments to small children, especially when the child is the boss's son. They were complimentary. Now I realize the importance of this positive aspect since I remember this as a pleasant happening. Had there been a negative aspect, I am sure that this would have given me a different outlook.

My father made deliveries too, and this was by horse and wagon. According to my mother, the bakery was very prosperous and making a lot of money. This aspect was apparent to others, particularly to a man with the last name of Schmidt who kept after my dad to sell him the business. My mother was strongly opposed to this; I am sure of it since I'd heard of this repeatedly for years. The culprit in this narration is alcohol since dad did a lot of drinking and working. It is very obvious that his judgment became distorted eventually, through the constant hounding by persistent Schmidt, father sold an apparent lucrative business for "peanuts."

I will try to recall my childhood days in the bakery to the best of my ability. But the memory gets frayed by the passing of time. It seems that the childhood was normal and pleasant since no bad memories come drifting back to me from the distant past. I remember playing with other children, boys and girls, together. One time we were playing doctor with the girls, and it was very interesting, even though none of us knew what we were doing. Later, being very young and naïve, I told my mother my most private organ hurt. She had an inspection and asked me a lot of questions. I answered as best as I could, and she advised me as only a mother could, caringly and lovingly.

There were two girls who lived next door whose last name was Chase. Their mother and father would put them to bed and go out someplace. They lived on the first floor, and their bedroom window faced the bakery side. They would often call me over; being just a little boy, I would accept their invitation to jump into bed with them. It was really cozy and motherly. One girl was named Louise (Chase), and she even came over to my home on 53rd years later to see me. I remember I was on my knees scrubbing the floor for my mother at the time. Her visit was flattering but also a bit unnerving. I don't think I saw her after that.

Mother told me that when I was very small, I thought thunderstorms were funny. I would laugh hilariously as the thunder and lightning crashed through the blackened skies. She recalled that I would buy her little presents if I got some money. It would be either a bar of soap or something else that cost a nickel or so. She always rewarded me with a big hug and kind words that made me feel good. While living at the bakery, I recall being very curious as to the nature of scientific things. I experimented with a piece of cloth that I soaped up to a mess of suds; then I placed it in the hot attic to dry and wanted to know what happened to all the bubbles when it dried out. When I retrieved the dry cloth, my small mind couldn't figure it out. I must have been about four years old at the time. There were other things I was curious about and conducted experiments, but the exact nature of them escapes me. I do recall that I was always curious in this respect.

One of the most dramatic events of my life would certainly be the scalding hot water incident. Some aspects of this incident make me reflect that there was certainly a reason for it and a greater power aware of it. Seeing as the prognosis of the eventual outcome didn't materialize as predicted. I recall the scalding happening, even though I was just four years old. Yet, I do not recall any unpleasantness or pain connected with it. This is very unusual since the human psyche is formed by identifying with events and circumstances. I have no fears due to this or anguish, just that it happened, and I am aware of it. I remember it very clearly to this day. Let me recount the tragedy in detail.

I needed some stick strike matches that were located on top of this old black cast iron stove. The stoves in those days weighed a ton, were more cumbersome and higher. To reach the matches, I had to pull myself up to the top shelf of the stove, where the matches were. On the top part of the stove, the part where you cooked, was a pot of boiling water. As I attempted to get up, my hand got a hold of the boiling pot, and it came cascading down on me like a pouring rainstorm of steam and hot water. My mother was very alert; she checked me as I lay on the floor, then she ran to the bakery and told my dad. He came running up with a pail of cooking oil, I presumed and spilled it all over me. I was taken to the hospital, where the doctor said that too much of my body was scalded and there was no chance for survival. I would die within six hours. According to my parents, a good part of my body had been scalded, including my face. Most of the time, the doctor is dead right (pardon the expression) when they diagnose a serious condition. When my mother heard this, she got on her knees at St. Alexis right in the hallway and prayed to Jesus that I would be spared. She said that a few nurses passed by and seemed to glance over in a smirk, or smile or in a dubious askance way. This may have been mother's own interpretation, but I remember her telling me that.

The gist of the matter is that I did recover. My recovery did not happen by the snap of the finger. The hospital stay lasted six weeks, and there was considerable treatment involved. The part that stands out in my mind is the regularity of pulling off the skin from my chest and legs. Again, I recall no pain. There was some pain, however, and the worst kind. You see, I was so lonely for my mother and father. I was so overjoyed to see them and always wanted them to take me home. To this day, when I hear a lonely train whistle pierce the darkness of the night as I lie in bed, my mind takes me back to the hospital room, and I feel so alone.

My dad was very handsome. He wrote that his face was scaled. There were not marks at all on his face. He only had scarring on the upper part of his chest. I did not see scaring his legs or arms. What a miracle. Back to dad.

God in his mercy spared me the physical pain, for I do not remember any of it. I only remember that it happened. Then He showed His power in my recovery and performed a miracle through His Son Jesus Christ. I think of this and realize that I should work for Him in my life. This is no easy task. I have mangled it many times through my reluctance and frailty of my humanity. This last statement is not a thrust at any type of humility but simply a repetition of St. Paul's and the war we fight within ourselves. I shall continue with my story. I recall my mother telling me that I had the wanderlust to just roam off at about five. Once I ended up on Harvard and East 71st Street. I had no knowledge of how to get back. A policeman found me and questioned me and thru this brought me back.

We must have moved out of the bakery sometime before I was sixteen because I was sixteen and living on East 53rd at the time of Peter's death. At any rate, that closes my account of my bakery days unless something comes to mind later. Oh yes, one more thing, my brother John was a good marble shooter and pegger. To explain this, to peg meant that one kid sat on the ground with legs spread apart. There was on colored marble as a target that you threw at, the first person who hit it kept all the other thrown marbles. John was good at it; he always let me keep the marbles he won, which made me very happy.

I was raised by my mother and dad, who were very Catholic. It was very evident by religious pictures and other moments. We went to church each Sunday and observed the rules of the church. Mother would also go to church on special days and was a devout woman. Her days were always full, and I don't know where she found all of the time to do all the things she did. We were poor; mother would buy material and sew my shirts and other clothing that I wore. When I went to school with the homemade clothing, there were some raised eyebrows, laughs, and snickers of ridicule. No one recognized her effort and sincerity, and willingness to try. These snickers didn't affect me that much since I don't remember any adverse effects from them.

When mother washed clothes, she would wash them by hand. All whites she would boil in a copper tub that was made for that purpose. When the clothing was clean, mother used a hand wringer mounted on the stationary tubs. I motorized it by turning the handle, and she fed in the clothing. There was no dryer available except the good old sunshine. The clothes were hung on a line either in the basement or outside, weather permitting. To whiten the whites as they boiled, mother added a substance called bluing, which came in a small bottle and was concentrated. This meant that two or three drops were sufficient.

Mother would iron all her washing by hand without the luxury of an electric iron. She had irons made of a heavy steel possible cast iron, and she had several of these, which she alternated onto and off the black stove that had either a coal or wood fire. When an iron cooled, it was put back on the stove to warm up again. She had a board with no legs and had it propped up on one sill and the other end on the table.

From the beginning, we had no refrigerator, so built in the basement, against the wall was this enclosure made of stone. It was square, about 5 feet tall, and 2 ½ feet square. It was hallowed in the middle for storage on the bottom part, and there was a place for ice on the top. This system was effective as long as the ice lasted. The iceman came around every day to replenish the supply. There was a card that the customer put in the window to let him know your order. Whichever way you hung the card, the figure on the bottom always indicated the weight of ice desired that day. Then the iceman would clamp his prongs into the ice with a tool that looked like oversize pliers, swing the ice up onto his shoulder and carry it into the house. They became very adept at this. Kids would follow the ice wagon in the summertime to mooch chips of ice. Myself included.

I don't want to lead you into believing that we lived in this archaic society forever. As time went by, mother got an electric iron, a refrigerator, and a washing machine. We had pipes running through the walls carrying natural gas, with jets coming out of the wall in certain spots. When the electricity failed during a storm or for some other reason, we lighted a gas jet for light. It gave an eerie appearance as the light danced unevenly on the wall of the room. There was a valve on each jet to adjust the amount of light required. You can imagine the dirt of the flame since we burnt straight raw gas.

The radio was an important part of the family. I remember my mother keeping her appointment with Don Amechi, who was on a program called "first nighter." It was sponsored by Campana's Italian Balm. I didn't know what that was and wondered why anyone would sell bombs. The program was romantic, and a young Don Amechi had the perfect voice for radio. Mother just loved that program. At the time, radios were made as furniture and rather elaborate; we had zenith with fantastic tone. The program I remember the most was put on by Firestone on Sunday night when they played beautiful relaxing music. This came on at about 8 o'clock in the evening. Sunday during the day was filled with radio drama of every description, murder, detective, mystery, romance. Then, later on, the big shows came on with the big bands. Hit Parade put on by Lucky Strike was very popular and had comedy by Jack Benny, Fibber McGee, and Molly, Jack Benny, Red Skelton, etc. By the way, I love the dramatizations on the radio and would lie on the couch listening for several hours. Sam Spade, the detective, was my favorite.

Later, we also had a record player, and my brothers and sisters and I would sit in the living room listening to the popular hits. Life was less complicated then. Just a glimpse of my family life at about age 12. I remember being in the living room with my sisters and brothers playing records on a graphophone. The modern-day version is called a record player. On ours, you had to crank it up to keep it running—many times in the middle of a song, it used to wind down and sounded funny. I still recall one song called "Valencia" and remember a lot of the melody.

I frequently worked jigsaw puzzles, but a lot of my time was spent outdoors with the other guys in the neighborhood. We played a game called arrows. A bunch of guys would get together and split into two groups. The first group would take off and hide away somewhere. After some elapsed time, we were supposed to track them down and bring them to a pre-designated place. The escaping team could separate and go in different directions, but they had to make an arrow on the sidewalk in the direction they went and an arrow when they made a turn. This game could last three to four hours and was a lot of fun.

At times, and as boys will be boys, we had our pranks. One prank we pulled could really psyche you out after a while, and I am sure there were many people left with a weird creepy feeling. The prank went like this: We took a safety pin, sneaked up on someone's porch, and stuck the pointed edge of the pin into the wood right next to the window. There was a strong piece of black string tied to the pin, and the string was drawn over into the bushes where we were hiding. Sharp pulls on the string would create a tapping on the window. We did this when it was dark, and it was hard to detect the source of this noise. The people would come out of the house to investigate the noise, and then we would stop, all the time giggling with nervous excitement and fear of being caught. We would repeat this several times and then move on to someone else's house before we would get caught. Believe me; it was a real accomplishment to just get on the porch to set the pin in position without getting caught.

There was a gag we pulled that could be termed malicious with the mentality we have with maturity, but at that time, it was fun. That is why when I look back on my youth, I feel I should find tolerance with today's youth since we did our share of stupid things. For instance, here is a dumb trick that we did that was a health hazard in addition to being potentially hazardous to physical health. Shock, too, could have resulted from this to a person with a weak heart.

We got two empty cans that were opened by an old-fashioned can opener. This meant that the tops were partially attached to the can. This was ideal for tying a string around the top of the can that stock menacingly upward with its jagged edge almost looking like teeth ready to bite. We would lower the cans into the sewer and fill them with sewer water. Then each can was placed on each side of the sidewalk with a black string tied from one can to another. The cans were placed in higher grass so as not to be detected. The string running across the sidewalk was not discernible in the dark since we used dark string. The object was for anyone walking the sidewalk to get drenched with this dirty water; what the shock it must have been. We always located this prank right by a ravine, and we would lay on the side of the hill peeking over. When people kicked the cans over, there was the usual dismay, anguish, and anger mixed with surprise. We could not help but laugh and run the risk of being chased, but it was easy getting away because rarely would anyone follow us through the ravine.

Pardon my jumping around as I go back to writing about the home I was raised in the conditions at that time. We lived in a six-room house with three bedrooms, a living room, dining room, kitchen, and basement. It was a full basement under the whole house. The dining room wasn't big, but it was adequate. The living room was smaller than it should be, and a couple of hooks here and there in the wall would have turned it into a big closet. We had a coal furnace, and mother made do with six tons of coal a year. This meant that the furnace went out at night, and we had better be in bed, or we would freeze to death. All of the water lines were insulated so they would not freeze. Mother in her mercy would always put a few paving bricks on the stove to heat them up, and when we went to bed, she wrapped them in a cloth, and we put our feet on them to keep warm. God bless her for this act of love. Mother was up early, and I could hear her as she tended the furnace, for she had adopted that job. Maybe by default. I wonder how she felt when it was bitter cold, and she got up to make the fire. She also cleaned out the ashes and carried the coal.

She loved flowers and had a garden full of them. The flowers were robust and healthy. You could see the loving care in their abundance and hearty beauty. My dad was a baker and a good one who really knew his stuff about being a manager of a bakery shop. This is why he always ended up being the boss in whatever place he worked. Dad had very little formal education if any. If he had the opportunity, he could have made a lot of progress in life. That is if he had changed his lifestyle, of course, since he did drink an awful lot of whiskey, and many times he barely made it home. At times this really did interfere with his job.

He was unemployed for long periods of time, and it certainly reflected in our lifestyle, which was bad enough already. Yet, when you are poor and never were rich or accustomed to the finer things, you really couldn't miss something you never had.

We had two large bedrooms upstairs, and dad and mom slept in the one-bedroom downstairs. The boys, Walter, John, Pete, and I, slept in the front bedroom toward the street side. Pete and I slept together, and John usually had his own bed. The girls, Frances, Helen, and Carrie, slept in the other two beds in the back room. The beds were made of steel, very sturdy, and had a spring system since there were no box springs or mattresses. Our mattress consisted of a mattress bag filled with the husks from corn. For the covers or quilts, mother would save the feathers from geese that we would have as food. She then would peel the stems away, and the soft down was left. This process took years, but they made fantastic covers, and I had a comforter made of pure goose down. They call them a "piezinia" in Polish. Some of the pillows were filled with chicken feathers, and they weren't too great because they matted up. The sleeping was good nevertheless since people can adjust to anything if we don't know any other way and there was nothing to compare.

When it was very cold, my sisters would ask me to go upstairs first and lay in their beds first to warm them up. Usually, I would, and then they would heap compliments on me for being so good. It had to be a con game, but I was catching on too late. Bugs were a problem at the time, mainly bedbugs. They bit hard and drew blood. Periodically I sterilized the bed with a hot blow torch or poured kerosene into hidden areas of the bed to destroy them. This controlled them, but they were had to get rid of. Going to bed, we had to go through the back door, up a stairway, and past a partly unfinished attic and various other places that were musty, weird, darkly secluded, and mysterious. This could play on a young mind. To top it off, if we were a little noisy, someone would come and pound on the outside door leading to the bedroom. They never announced who it was, and it was a terrifying experience. Sometimes I felt trapped and felt like going out the front window to escape. This escape would have involved jumping off the front porch roof. Don't think I didn't consider it just to escape that trapped feeling. This leaves a lasting effect on the psyche, and I would attribute this as a cause of my claustrophobia that I experience in certain areas.

Other things I did as a child. In days past, they had root beer stands with frosty glasses and a creamy textured root beer that no longer exists today. The nearest stand from my home on 53rd was on Broadway Avenue, right where the Ann Vogue dress shop was located. The deal was all you could drink for a nickel. We would save up a nickel walk down there, making sure it was a very hot day, plunk down the nickel and load up. Boy was that good, and the deal was legitimate as long as you drank it there.

When there was no one around to play with, I would crawl or climb onto our garage, hauling up a lot of pretty good-sized stones with me. The game's object was to lie very quietly on the roof in a prone position and watch for rats to come out of the garage or the neighbor's barn. There were plenty of rodents around, and they weren't too cautious. The rats would come out, and the object was to time a rock in flight to see if I could make a direct hit. It was sort of a bombing mission. Sometimes I made some pretty good hits.

Some of the things we did for amusement or entertainment would be in order to relate at this time. Down in the ravine, we had a big swing on the side of a steep hill. The rope was tied up on a distance branch and connected onto an automobile tire in which we sat. Someone would give a big push, and off we would go into nothing but space. This was a real thrill; we never realized the propensity of danger.

We would go into the woods and find a young tree that had a crooked root. With care, we would take the tree out of the ground, and if we were successful, it turned out to be a hockey stick. All the kids did this, and then we played hockey in the street. A can of condensed milk served as a hockey puck, and the road served as the field. One time in a heated moment of play, I swung hard at the puck and missed, but my upward swing hit my brother Pete right in the mouth and split his lips. Blood was all over, and I got scared, especially when he ran home to tell Ma. I didn't go home that night until about ten, hoping that the situation would cool by then. It was an accident, but my young mind could only conceive a punishment, so I tried to lay low. Oh yes, there was no punishment.

My childhood days were during the lean depression years. There was prohibition, which many blamed in part for some of the depression woes. It also was the cause of much crime due to so-called bootlegging. It was the era of the big-time crook or gangsters, and the headlines were seldom devoid of a headline screaming the crime of public enemy number one. These were the days of Al Capone, pretty boy Floyd, Dillinger, Filkowski, and other enemies of society. When prohibition ended in 1933, there was supposed to be a new era of prosperity. The song "Happy Days are Here Again" became popular, and it was not uncommon to see someone drinking a glass of beer and singing that song. The depression may have ended for some people, but for me, there was no appreciable difference. There wasn't much need for a lot of money. My goals, similar to other kids, revolved around the bare minimum of about five cents. Five cents opened the door to many avenues for a nickel's worth had a realistic value in those days. Saturday afternoon movies were five cents. For this, you could see your favorite cowboy and get a glossy 10x12 picture of him. There was Tom Mix with his wonder horse,

Hoot Gibson, Tim McCoys, Roy Rogers, and Gene Autrey a little later on. Hop along, Cassidy was a big favorite, and at that time, a German police dog was a big star. Rin-Tin-Tin.

Another thing that was a nickel was good for was an ice cream cone with a double scoop. Also, there were grab bags that sold for a penny, another thing that stayed in that price line. (a grab bag is a bag full of older candy that the storekeeper wants to get rid of) Chocolate bars were sold for 25 cents for a pound bar.

Money was hard to come by, and we did many things to pick up a few pennies. There were many places that people would just dump their rubbish and whatnot; we could forage through the dump for old rags, metal, and newspapers. We looked until we could acquire an amount that we had the purchasing power to buy some of the things I mentioned. Since there was no such thing as an allowance, it was up to us to get our own money. Once I tried all week to save up four cents for a cowboy movie I wanted to see Saturday. I told my mother about it and that I needed was one more penny to get to see the film. She gave me a positive "No" answer. I reasoned that if I worked on her long enough, she had to give in. I followed after crying and begging for what seemed like an awfully long time, but after all that, the answer was still "No." From that time on, when mother said no to me, I knew she meant it. I didn't bother nagging her because that would be a waste of time. I knew that she would walk long distances just to save a penny, and it wasn't that she was stingy or miserly but purely out of necessity. You know, even to this day, I wish she would have given me that penny because I really loved those cowboy shows. I do not wish to infer that we were never given any money, this must of happened sometimes. My dad drank a lot; often, he had money. Who wouldn't try to work him for a touch in his weakened condition? Mother would go through his pockets and salvage what she could while the beer joint was the big winner.

There was an aluminum smelting factory on Harvard Avenue, where they melted the aluminum out of this clay (bauxite). They would gather the melted aluminum in quantity and dump the rest of the soil in their dump. We kids would go down the side of a hill, sometimes sliding down since the soil was still loose. We were looking for nuggets of aluminum, and they were there in various sizes. When we accumulated a fair amount, we would sell them to the ragman, who came down the street periodically with his horse and wagon shouting "PaPa, Rags," which means paper and rags.

Another way we got spending money was not strictly legal according to the law, but believe me, we were pretty honest and did not steal with any malicious intent. On Grand Avenue at the farthest end of the street and bordered by 49th Street was the milk bottle redemption center. Milk used to be delivered in glass bottles at that time, and you paid a deposit on the bottle. The deposit price was embossed right on the bottle. There were some 2 cent markings or 5 cent makings that stood out almost like a screaming voice saying, "Hey, look, I'm five cents, the price of a Saturday movie." The bottle would be lying on a pile of glass inside a high fence at the redemption center. The purpose of this place was that when a bottle had chip or was cracked, they were sent here to be redeemed and then destroyed. They would be thrown on this pile of glass but at times would not break any further except for a chip or two. We would scout out the bottles to see if there were any good ones on the pile. If there were ones that looked good enough, we would jump the fence, grab the bottle and then hurry back over the fence. Then we would run like heck since there always was a policeman there patrolling, and he would chase us. There were also patrol cars, so we really had to be on alert. Once we made our getaway, the bottle was taken to the store to be redeemed for the money it was worth.

SCHOOL DAYS

To give you some background of my days at school, I will begin with my abbreviated days at Immaculate Heart. These were the days that Catholic Schools had only nun teachers. I said abbreviated days because I did not last long in the Catholic school system. The nuns were very strict and made me write right-handed. Their method of punishment was to slap the palms of the hands with a rubber hose. I think this in itself, whether justified or not, was brutal. Yet, this is not really meant to be a condemnation of the nuns since I realize now that I was no angel. This will be born out later, in different parts of my narration.

I am writing all of this right-handed because when I went to Catholic school, the nuns forced me to write right-handed. When I went back to left-handed, they cracked my knuckles with a ruler.

The outstanding thing I remember about Catholic school is the free dental service. Periodically, a doctor would come to school for free dental examinations. They would then set up a dental office right at school and repair all the teeth that needed to be repaired. The methods at that time were very archaic yet very effective since the fillings lasted a very long time and never fell out. The method used was that noisy old drill that felt like a jack-hammer and then installing the filling. The filling was pressed into position with some kind of pick, like a nut pick, but then they secured with something like a center-punch and a big rubber mallet. The dentist pounded the filling into the tooth, shaking up your whole head and body. The dentist complimented me on being a very good patient. He was so impressed that I was escorted from classroom to classroom, and all the kids were told what a brave little boy I was. They were apparently having a lot of trouble with the other kids, and I am sure their presentation had to be a very big psychological factor. Anyway, this kind of makes you feel like a hero, especially to a little boy who didn't seem to have much going for him and wasn't even aware of it.

Yet my days at Immaculate Heart didn't last too long because I kept telling my mother how bad it was at that school, and I finally convinced her that I should be transferred to Washington Park School. When this happened, I don't recall, but it had to be in an early grade because Washington Park School is an elementary school. When the school tested me, I was moved back half a grade or maybe a whole grade. At any rate, it resulted in my graduating from high school a year later. This in itself leaves a mark on a person since I felt that I couldn't be too smart because I was demoted a full grade. Before it escapes my memory, at the time, this became my complex number two. First, the scalding scars affected me feeling different from other people, and now I am set back a grade in school. These lend themselves to lower self-esteem. I wasn't aware that the Catholic school was deficient academically and hadn't covered all the material. Yet, the impression of not feeling too bright lasted until I got to Myron T. Herrick. It was called Fowler when I got there, and then they changed the name later to Herrick. More about Herrick later. There are a few stories to relate about Washington Park School before I get into my junior high school days.

The repercussions developed slowly but snowballed where it did affect me. One example of the scars was that I refused to take off my shirt.

49

I absolutely would not go swimming on a public beach because I was sure people would stare at me and laugh. It even bothered me later as I thought no woman would want to marry me because she would have to touch those ugly scars. Many people have hang-ups like this, and it would be good if they could talk them out and clarify them instead of bending their imaginations all out of shape.

At Washington Park School, I recall that my conduct had to be bad since there were trips to the principal's office and spankings with a huge yardstick. I don't know if this was the norm or not because I never felt I was ever that bad. It just seemed that I saw things differently and got into trouble over it.

A fact that just returned to me that could have influenced my life and obviously retarded my growth was that I only spoke Polish until I was five years old. My mother and father always talked in Polish, and I was caught in the stream of things. This is odd since mother did speak English well enough. She came to this country when she was three years old. Well, at any rate, it is increasingly evident that my life isn't starting out on the right foot.

Getting back to Washington Park School, I had my first love affair there. I fell in love with my teacher Miss Pearson. She was the first kind and understanding authority figure that I encountered, and she made me feel like something. My second love affair originated in Fowler's Junior High, and again, it was my teacher, Miss Liebowitz. At this time, the reasons were a little different, for I readily recall that she was pretty and really stacked. Slowly manhood was stirring within me.

When I refer to Miss Pearson as the first kind and understanding authority figure, I mean one of the few I could identify with. There was no intention to convey an impression that everyone was bad and opposed to me. But remember, here we are dealing with a very poor son of immigrants, and you can read into some of the confusion and defensiveness I had at that time. We of that era lived an entirely different lifestyle than the lifestyle of this era.

SPENDING MONEY

At times we foraged in the dump for junk to sell to the ragman. You would come across one discarded skate whose wheels looked pretty good. This automatically became a scooter of sorts, which we called "a chitty."

(Editor's note: years later, they were called skateboards) The skate could be separated into two sections at the point of the adjustment for either longer or shorter. I would find a two by four, perhaps two feet long, and nail the two parts of the skate onto the two by four. One section would go on the front, and one would go on the back.

I would then go to the grocer for an orange crate that seemed to be always available and nail the crate onto the two by four, making it the front side. Onto the crate were nailed two pieces of wood on each side of the top to act as handles, and believe me, it made a very good scooter that went fast and was a lot of fun.

A GIFT FOR ME

To buy a toy in our family was impossible since we needed all the money to live on. I recollect having one toy that I cherished dearly. It was given to me by my Aunt Frances (Scionka, one of my mother's sisters). This was a little wooden boat that I just loved and valued like it was golden. I would float it in the bathtub and during or after a rainstorm.

When not in use, I would hide it under my mother's bed or in a dresser drawer way in the back so no one would take it. This, I'm sure, gave me my sense of appreciation and formed values in me. Yet, there is also a possibility of adopting frugal tendencies through your life that could border on miserly. Yet, these experiences are valued since we learned to work for what we wanted, and nothing was owed us except the basics for living. This truly was "no-frill," living in the purest sense.

GOVERNMENT AID

In these depressed times, the government had federal aid for those grossly in need. They would distribute government surplus in the form of flour, beans, etc. I would accompany my mother with a wagon and carry those items home. This distribution center was on Harvard Avenue just above E. 42nd Street. The government had taken over a huge building that the underworld had previously used as a big gambling establishment.

At that time, this place was replete with all forms of gambling, and up by the ceiling were small holes where gunmen stood guard with sub-machine guns. The barrel-end of the gun jutted out of these holes. The building today, or rather where it was located, is now the site of the huge J.L. Goodman warehouse. (1986)

MARATHON

The area I just mentioned brings back many memories since, in that immediate area, there had been the Marathon and the Taylor Bowl. To explain this, I shall start with the Marathon. There was this big hall the size of an auditorium, later used as the Harvard Club and later by the government for surplus distribution. Dance couples would volunteer to dance as long as possible, with a break in between but only if the other partner stayed on the floor. I think that is the way that was. Anyway, the object was to see who could outlast who. This went on for days until the couple who remained won the first prize.

People paid money to see this, and they would put on different shows in between. This, too, was done during the depression. I attended one Marathon as a spectator, and it was pitiful the way the people dragged around. I was young too at that time, and besides, I didn't know how to dance. The Taylor Bowl was an arena built farther back of the same area. It was built as the name infers: like a bowl that had seats running all around in a circle, like any arena, really. The only difference is that it had NO ROOF, and they built up the walls with corrugated steel sheets—the same type of sheets used today on some roofs on farm barns. The purpose of the arena was for sporting events, but mainly boxing since there was a permanent ring in the area's center.

We kids didn't have any money to pay our way, so we would sneak in. We would find a section of corrugated metal that was a little loose and sneak under it. Mr. Taylor, who owned the bowl, had a nice-looking daughter, but I only discovered this later when I went to high school. She and I went out together a few times, but I don't know what caused us to part. I failed to mention in the story about the Marathon that Red Skelton, a famous American entertainer/comedian was there later on when he was just starting in his career.

MORE EARNING SCHEMES

I hope that this narration is not mumble jumble and somewhat interesting, since a lot of effort and time is being spent on it. Also, I skip around a little because a memory will come back to me, and then I write it right away, so I don't lose it again. So, I will relate another way that I spent my time trying to make some money. Out on Schaff Road (Brooklyn Hts.) were many farms that raised a variety of vegetables. My friends and I would get up early in the morning and go to some of these farms seeking employment.

One morning, I was hired to pick beans (string beans). The rate was fifty cents a *day*, for a very *long* day. I picked them on my knees all day long in that hot sun, and I still remember that as being a very long day. Maybe that's why I don't LIKE green beans even to this day. They fertilized the soil with the waste from the sewage disposal. The waste has a lot of broken glass in it, and at the end of the day, boy, my knees were cut up and sore. This is one job that I gave up on and fast.

We kids would wander off toward the Schaff Road area often since there were many hills and valleys there with plenty of trees and grass. The canal ran through there, and we would have a spot to swim picked out a nice, wide area. There was some risk involved since there were a lot of snakes around. I was in the water, looking right, even with the surface of the water, when I saw this snakehead swimming right along toward me. You never saw me move any faster than that as I vacated the premises. These snakes had a yellow diamond on their head and looked kind of menacing, but we put up with them.

Near Schaaf Road was a series of railroad tracks that ran through and connected to the industrial valley. There were steel mills there and other industries in that locale. In our exploits, we would wander around all over for hours and, of course, get pretty hungry at times.

RAILROAD TRESTLE

One time, we were near a farmer's field that was full of ripe tomatoes. Being hungry will sort of dull your conscience to an extent. So, in these weaker moments, we decided to "borrow" a few tomatoes to quench our hunger and thirst. We got the tomatoes, stuffed them in our shirts, and took off as the farmer started to come after us. We were on the opposite side of the train trestle, and the only way to get back was over this trestle.

It was just a bridge for trains to cross over the valley. There were two sets of tracks for trains coming and going. On the bridge were built a few small alcoves to step off into if a train was coming. The bridge's elevation was very high, and it was a long way down, indicating if anyone fell off, sure death, I'm sure.

The bridge was very long too and shook like it could fall apart with a train on it. Here I was with a shirt full of tomatoes, the farmer coming at top speed, and me heading for the trestle to get to the other side! There was a walkway between the sets of tracks, and I was running at top speed on this walkway. I heard train whistles come out of nowhere, and the least desirable thing was about to happen to me. I was about to be caught in the middle of the trestle, with two trains crossing at the same time and me in the middle. There wasn't time to get into the alcove, so I laid down on the walkway holding on for dear life.

Those two trains were rolling by me on both sides, steaming, hissing, and shaking every wooden board in that bridge's structure. I felt this was IT and that the wind or the suction would draw me in. It was my own eternity, and I must have learned to pray right there. There I was, holding on for dear life, scared to death, laying in all these squashed tomatoes! Thank God those trains passed, and I got out of there.

CHURCH, DISCOVERING GOD, and SNAKES

Thus far, I have been enumerating some of the events of my young life. There are some things written that might suggest that I was a bad boy, but if it does, it was never with malice. Some might say it doesn't sound so bad, which might be a comparison to theirs. At any rate, a variety of opinions will be formed according to whoever reads this and their interpretation. This is immaterial to me. What is material to me is that I should like to inject some balance into these writings.

God was always aware of me as He is of all His created creatures. There was a steady ritual of me going to church thru my young life, and it really didn't turn me on, but Mom said I would go, and I went. This was every Sunday; I fulfilled an obligation that I didn't ever know I was obligated to, or why. There is a Bible passage that reads, "If today you hear his voice, harden not your heart." Since we are all His people, He will enlighten us from time to time to lead us on His way.

The "Harden not our heart" section indicates that you may exercise your own will. There was a particular Sunday that I went to church at the age of eight, and whereas I must have heard many sermons before that, this is the first one that a particular thing the priest said stuck in my mind and caused me to think.

He was quoting the First Commandment and the Second Commandment. The part that motivated my thought process was that God was telling me to love Him with my entire being. This is enormously heavy stuff for a little boy who really wasn't paying much attention to this "God Talk." This day, however, was different. I became aware for the first time, and to become aware, plant a seed. Now, when I went to church, I wasn't overwhelmed, nor was I dramatically converted, but I did listen, but only once in a while.

I learned that a child's mind has a short span and takes everything as it is said. When they told me Satan was a snake, I believed all snakes were from Satan. This prompted a couple of other kids and me to go into the dump, catch a snake, and chop it to pieces. This reptile, to me that represented evil. My learning of God evolved slowly and over a long span of time and continues to this day, and I thank him for his patience with all of His creatures.

CREEK

Here was this big field in the back of my mother's home that belonged to Mr. Komorowski. That was only a small part of the area. The land went right back out to this big valley that was a veritable forest. In the valley were two creeks that both ran from south to north. One creek we called "rusty creek" because of its "rusty" reddy color, which today undoubtedly had to be contamination from some industry. The other creek had a gray or a dirty milky look and also was contaminated. This creek carried away a lot of sewage from the city. We detected and suspected this was the case from some of the objects floating in the water. Being kids, however, we did not dwell on a subject like water purity, and the adult world was unconcerned about it too. This creek, or both creeks, was a source of fun to us since we would go down in the valley and play a game called "jumping creeks." The game was just what the name implied. One kid would challenge another to jump a certain section of a creek, and whichever one stepped in the water or fell in the mud was the loser.

CATCHING RATS

We would try several spots, and at the end, the guy with the most complete jumps was the winner. There was another game we played called "catching rats." We would locate some rat holes along the side of the creek. We knew through experience that a rat doesn't just dig one hole. He has an entrance hole, an exit hole, and an escape hole. He also does not dig straight down, but digs down and then up, and forms a sort of water trap, that if it should flood excessively and water ran into the hole, it wouldn't flood them out right away.

We would get a bucket of water and pour water down the main hole; it took an awful lot of water. One kid would watch a hole apiece, with a club in his hands, while the other kid kept pouring water down the main hole. The expectation was like electricity, especially when we could see water coming into the other holes and knew the rat was hell-bent on escape. Suddenly there was a stirring of the water and a gurgling type sound, and we KNEW the rat was on his way. Now you only get one chance to hit him with the club. There was a limited success to this "game," but the fun had already been accomplished whether we caught him or not.

COOK-OUT

In this area was a natural spring that had fantastic water to drink. It wasn't necessary ever to go home for a drink of water. This water was cool, clearly clean, and almost sparkled invitingly to all people of the area. Some people came with gallon jugs to carry the water away. The water came in very handy right after one of our "cook-outs." The "cook-out" consisted of getting a potato from home and going into the "dump" or ravine, building a fire, and cooking the potato. There were two options, either put the potato into the fire as is and "cook it" until a black coat formed on it about a quarter-inch thick. The other was to find some grey clay, which was easily found, wrap it in clay, and bake it. Either way; the potato tasted delicious since we already were starved by the time they were done. My preference was the potato with the black shell since it seemed to have more taste to it. The clay-baked potato came out really clean-----and----really HOT!

ADVENTURES

As I proceed with this narration, which takes on the aspects of desultory (random, lacking a plan, etc.) ramble, I know it couldn't be any other way since I write things that just come to mind and put them down before they escape me. Like the time in Raus Park (Brow Avenue/Newburgh Hts.) (this is the area behind my mother's home, which was an amusement park, but before my time). The two-story building was the remaining reminder of that park, and a metal ring that was flat and looked like a track that could have been a merry-go-round was the only remains of those by-gone days. Inside the building, there were clay statues resembling an array of numerous figures, but they strangely lacked color and were all white only.

Peering through the window, they presented a rather eerie view for young eyes. The building was situated right on top of a rather long hill that ran into the valley. Facing the hill was a huge front porch making up the front of the second floor of the building. We kids managed to get up on that porch to drop things off of it. On one occasion, we discussed cats having nine lives and wanted to find out if that were true.

We took an automobile tire, put a cat in it, and dropped him from the porch. Well, when the cat hit the ground, he lost all interest in our experiment. We knew that he had extra lives anyway. Now, this is really a weird thing to do, but for the sake of an honest narration, I must include all of these incidents. This should give parents a better concept of some of the things boys think and do and grow in a better understanding of the immature mind.

There was a limited amount of automobiles at that time, and I lived in Newburgh Hts., which always seemed to be broke and operated on limited funds. Nothing has changed with any of these municipalities that are still broke. They had a volunteer fire department. It consisted of a huge cart that had a lot of fire hose rolled upon it; on the front end, there were two long poles that one horse could fit in to pull the contraption. I never did see the horse, but when the alarm went off for a fire drill, we would rush to the corner of E. 53rd Street where the hose was located and practice pulling this thing up the street to a hydrant and going through the motions.

In those days, there were many sandlot baseball, perhaps a lot more than today. Washington Park was very busy with games from early morning into the late afternoon. The park had two diamonds, numbers one and number two. They played ball mainly on Sunday. One of my main activities was to hang around the groundskeeper until all the baseball was over, just to help him carry the base bags back, and he gave a tip. He carried the bags back to the main storehouse about 600 feet away. He didn't need the help, but he rewarded me for my patience to wait that long for a tip. There was just enough money to buy a Butterfinger candy bar, which I just loved. Butterfingers at that time were much larger and very filling and satisfying for a little boy.

The baseball field was located off the boulevard in the back of where the tennis courts are still located today (1986). The backstop tried to cover the ravine located in back of it, but there was an occasional foul ball that went flying off into the dump. When we needed a baseball, which was most of the time, we would wait on top of the hill for the foul to go over and down. We would chase it, and if we were fast enough, step it into the mud which was always present down there, hoping that no one would find it. When everyone left, we would dig it out, wash it, dry it out, and then have a real live baseball to play with.

You should know that there was *no* money to buy a baseball, and this baseball was used until we literally knocked the cover off of it. At times I would re-sew the threads, but the cover got so bad after a while that we used black tape to hold the ball together. We organized street teams and had regularly scheduled games. We traveled long distances at times to meet an opposing team.

Sometimes when we wanted to play a game and had no ball, we would let the kid play who had one. He usually had no talent, but we had no choice. Now the trick was to keep the kid happy because if he got mad, he would take his ball home, and this would ruin the game. The sad part was that the kid knew this and took advantage of it. When we had enough baseball, we'd tell him to get lost to get even.

DUMB THINGS

Now to the carnival. There were many wheels of chance and plenty of participants. One evening, some of my relatives played the wheel, my brother-in-law Joe and my brother Walter. They suspected that the man at the wheel was cheating, and they finally accused him of it. This built up into a great crescendo, and all hell broke loose. There was a real riotous fight, and I got out of the way because it looked like it was strictly for adults. The police came and stopped the fighting, and the carnival was closed down for the night.

One of the features of a carnival that came to town still lives in my mind very vividly. This was a highlight to attract attention and was in progress for either six or eight hours to keep people there. This is the way it was set up. There was a makeshift platform like a stage. The stage was about 12 feet wide and 12 feet deep. It was made of wood and upraised off the ground about 36 to 40 inches, high enough so everyone could see. This event was pre-advertised and drew a lot of people. On the stage was a hypnotist, a swami-type person, representing someone from the orient or the far east. There was another person with a turban who the hypnotist was supposed to hypnotize. Next to them was a coffin into which the person to be hypnotized went. After a lot of hula-balu and a tremendous buildup, the victim appeared to be in a state of sleep. They nailed the coffin shut and put him in a grave that was already dug. We were all invited to inspect the coffin and the grave, which isn't something you do every day. They then shoveled the dirt into the hole, and they specified the length of time the body would remain buried. It was at least 6 hours that he stayed in the ground, then they started digging frantically to get him out of there to give the appearance that something was wrong. With haste, they pulled the coffin from the ground and brought it back on stage. They proceeded to pull the nails out of the top and stood the coffin upright, revealing this person who made you wonder if he was dead or alive. The hypnotist always seemed to have difficulty arousing the person, but at long last, he always succeeded. This was very exciting to see.

Once I was walking down Lansing Avenue, but not in a conventional way. I was walking along the curb looking for gum wrappers (Wrigley's). They were supposed to have a series of numbers inside the wrapper that held some importance at that time. To this date, the element of that importance escapes me. I had just gone down E. 65th Street and turned the corner of Orey Avenue looking for those wrappers.

Suddenly, a car came around the corner and headed right for me. I had the option of getting hit, for I couldn't get out of the way in time. I opted to jump up onto the hood of the car and avoided getting hurt, possibly badly. The man was nice about it and made a big deal of it, even took me home and told Mom about it. I wasn't really hurt, though, just scared. This taught me to be a little more careful now.

I must tell you about the old telephone building, the alleged haunted building across the street from it, and the big scare of the shining tombstones, but let's do it one at a time.

A building was partly demolished on E. 49th Street on the same side of the street as the Newburgh Hts., Town Hall, and about 600 feet away from it. As rumors go, or get started, someone suggested that the building is haunted, and then the rumor spreads like a grass fire in a high wind. Before much time transpired, they even had the police believing it. There was an investigation of the premises to dispel and squelch these tales that were turning into pseudo-fact—the entire Newburgh Heights Police force made their investigation (three strong) and came out with the conviction that this was all a farce.

However, they may have been a little dubious. They entered with guns drawn, perhaps to alleviate a bit of skepticism that lingered in their collective minds. There was a relieved expression on their faces as they came out of the building, rather quickly, I thought. Yet, to the imaginative mind of a youth, who seeks excitement and scratches for adventure, this demonstration was not conclusive. The youthful brain trust of the neighborhood remained unconvinced. After a high-level meeting of three or four *kids*, we decided that there *had* to be a ghost in that building, and the only way to find out was to hold our own in investigation.

The idea of the investigation was formulated quickly, but the formation of the investigating team took a lot longer. Now I seldom win anything, and I'm not that good in elections for office or anything of a lucrative nature, but every one of these kids was convinced that *I* should be part of the investigating team. This election was prompt, concise, and instant.

There were two other courageous souls who were dubiously elected to go on this *journey into the unknown*. Now, it was important to follow through because the term for anyone reneging is called "chicken" and never would be lived down.

We started toward the opening, which at one time had been a door, with all types of thoughts that send an icy terror into our hearts. Hesitatingly, we went one slow step at a time and entered into piles of rubble of bricks, and cement, dust, and rubbish, and pools of dirty water that attested to previous rain. Directly ahead was a stairwell in surprisingly good shape, and it was the object of our course of action since we had to go to the third floor, where some man had hung himself. (Rumor) The broken pieces of stone on the stairway, coupled with the rubbery trepidation of our legs, made for a slow upward climb, not that we were rushing headlong into this, even without that handicap.

In the pitiful broken-down condition of this building, even the slightest shadow seemed to rear its ugly head. Paradoxically, the thrill was there for three little dirty-faced kids with a yearning for adventure but no knack for heroics. To achieve this, we were willing to have the blood run cold in our veins and have our imaginations wreak havoc with the little serenity we *did* possess. In the fantasyland of the young boy, we could almost feel the icy fingers of the skeleton that was about to clutch us in an unbreakable grip.

All of these thoughts crashed through our minds and bodies as we approached the sinister third floor. Suddenly, there was a noise, all our trials and tribulations turned to action as we flew down the stairs and into the safe outdoors! This story was a conversation piece for years, and as the years grow, so did the distortion of the story.

The old telephone building I mention was abandoned and was six stories high. There was a flat roof on the building with a trap door in the middle that could be pulled up with some effort. Inside the building were rolls of lead that were used for insulation on telephone lines. Some of the other older kids would climb the metal ladder on the building's side, get on the roof and pry open the trap door. Then they would drop down and throw out what metal they could to sell to the ragman. We never did this and didn't steal in a malicious sense, only a milk bottle or a tomato, etc. Never to be thieves for the sake of being a thief. These older guys planted a seed, and there was another challenge presenting itself, a challenge needing to be fulfilled.

All of the valid reasons for *not* doing that were simply ignored, and there were many. For instance, the police frowned on such activity. The building was condemned; this was an act of trespassing. The iron ladder was loose on the building's side since the cement that held it was old and crumbly. If *this* wouldn't be sufficiently deterring, the building was right next to the police station, and it would take a phantom to get to the top undetected. We were not too adept at this sort of thing, but facing all the odds of inexperience, fear, and stupidity, we proceeded with a nonchalant type of reckless abandon.

Others went up ahead of me, and their urgings as I climbed up was disturbing, coupled with the loose uncertainty of the ladder and the height involved. We all got to the top, and as soon as we did, the cops appeared on the scene. They knew all the time but didn't want to distract any of us while we were in transit to avoid a disaster of a fatal fall. Now they commanded us to come down, and we, in typical hoodlum fashion, said, "Come up and get us, coppers!" This phrase certainly was not original but direct from the movies. The gangster picture was very popular at that time, and the gangster was a somewhat questionable hero: this we tried to emulate.

REFLECTION

Boys are very impressionable and carry these things out in their actions. It doesn't mean they are bad, but it does get them recognition, which is a by-product of love. To arrive at this love takes many devious avenues, especially to a youthful mind. That is why I feel that I developed some compassion and understanding of kids since they just experience many things in their incomplete state. This is not to infer that adults ever reach this full maturity, but only higher levels, whereas others hardly progress. This is not judgment or condemnation but a simple fact I arrived at by observation. These calculated thrills of anticipation are acceptable and enjoyable, however, usually more so in retrospect than in the actual process of happening. When unnecessary thrills are thrust upon you without any expectation or preparation, this is a horse of another color.

RAVINE

As a boy in elementary school, I found it convenient to cross across the ravine on the way to school, home for lunch, and back home after school. These trips were by and large uneventful, except for a muddy shoe or a scratch from a branch. But one day, there was a different event, very different, not planned, and terrifying to me that I recall vividly to this day and don't relish this ever happening again.

Coming home from school, I cut through the ravine as usual. My course took me up through the hills, and as I approached my very last hill, I climbed up to the top. I stepped onto flat land, which was full of high grass, and there was this massive colony of snakes! It would be impossible to guess their number, but they resembled a bowl of moving spaghetti, yet my momentum was so fast that I just missed ending up in the very middle of all the snakes! My course changed in a hurry, or faster than that.

The sight sent chills running through me and my heartbeat against my chest at a steady rate. Yet, after reaching what I considered a safe distance away from these snakes, I regained my composure and decided to have another look, but with caution. Sneaking back somewhat gingerly, I was amazed to find that all the snakes had vacated the premises, and the only trace left was the flattened grass in a rounded pattern. I didn't linger for an encore and made haste homeward.

REFLECTION

In everyone's life are high and low points. Joys and sorrows. Some people see nothing but the negative aspect of life, and this, hand in hand with self-pity, enhances negative attitudes that make life drudgery and something to be endured. Whereas others find a challenge to the little episodes, both good and bad, and generate a vigor to exhilaration as they meet the enemy of trial and a feeling of vigorous anticipation as they meet the joys. None the less, there is an adventure in life if only we can construe it as such.

RAVINE GHOST

For example, a woman was on her way home one summer evening. She was walking along E. 55th Street, heading toward Harvard Avenue. It was evening, and the street lights with poor intensity cast an eerie shadow across the path of her journey. The night had a darkness of inky intensity, a condition that could generate anticipation and cause fears that are normal to escalate to a crescendo of morbid fear.

We can only imagine her feeling on that particular night, but it is logical to assume that she had apprehension under these normal conditions. As she proceeded on her way, casting furtive glances in all directions, the streets were entirely deserted. Also adding to the loneliness of the situation and almost suggesting a situation of impending doom. The psyche carries a progressiveness about itself and can escalate into a panic that makes one fearful of the fear.

Assuming that our lady of this incident was experiencing these feelings, we can see her walking along with a hurried step, seeking to arrive at her safe sanctuary in the shortest possible time.

So the scene is set for events to follow, events that leave an indelible mark, knife into the brain, and after a prolonged period of recovery. Leave a scar that remains a constant reminder of that unforgettable night. The section of E. 55th that our lady was walking on that eventful night had formerly been a ravine that was spanned by a creaky wooden bridge, whose planks became progressively looser with time, and had a suggestion about itself that its safety was suspect. Since then, the gully had been filled by the city's refuse and garbage, and after settling, this road was built through it.

Located in just about the center of where the bridge had been, and as you stood on the bridge itself, looking out, you saw a wide expanse of the ravine, approximately 200 feet across. The ravine extended itself to the other side and went on and on. The ravine section that plays an integral part of this story is the section extending 2000 feet. At that point, the land was flat and even and housed a cemetery in that immediate area. As you walked along, you could view the cemetery markers very clearly, with their polished appearance and silent testimony.

With a quickened step, the lady had reached this point in her journey and, still exercising vigilant looks in all directions, suddenly saw a form of pale light in the shape of an identifiable ghost. And that moment struck piercing fear into her heart, which seemed to be pumping ice water into her heart suddenly. Needless to say, her steps became hurried and frenzied as she lunged toward her destiny. After arriving home, words came tumbling forth with incoherency, which added to the confusion of the moment. It was a considerable time before her conversation took on any aspects of cogency (being clear), and her spouse learned about this awesome specter she had observed.

Communication in that period was slower then and amounted to the telegraph, telephone, and "tele woman." This prompted the spread of this news like wild-fire, and the whole community's interest was aroused. The following night, hundreds of people assembled in the area looking for verification of this appalling report. I was there too and didn't know what to expect, but I went with some hesitation that was overshadowed by a compelling curiosity that refused to be quenched.

The police were represented as well, and the final determination was that the light's reflection was creating the "ghost" on the lamppost to the polished stone in the cemetery. The faint light barely made it to the stone but was sufficient to cause a reflection that was misty in appearance. The realism of the "ghost" was compounded simply because the stone was shaped in the form of a head and body and can be viewed to this day!

The situation was corrected by inserting a piece of cardboard into the light on the cemetery side, nullifying the reflection. This, my friends, was a real-life adventure! There are other adventures in life which can change what appears to be a mundane existence into a more abundant life.

MEDICINE SHOW

In the time of my youth, we had an event called a Medicine Show. No doubt, this show is a carry-over from the old West that we see in the movies occasionally. This show was a rather small operation with a closed van-type vehicle resembling a big truck with closed insides.

The Medicine Show truck rode up and down the streets and maybe played music, but they did something to arouse the populace to attend their show. They would specify the show's location and the hour, and at the appointed time. A good-sized crowd would form, and the shows were always pretty good. There would be different acts and a comic running a reasonable span of time. In between came the pitch for the medicine they were selling, which was usually hawked as a cure-all for all illnesses. I would guess that the medicine contained a lot of alcohol, and this in itself would give you a feeling of being cured –for a while.

Well, anyway, I never heard of anyone getting sick on the stuff, and it probably was as good as what you buy stuff off the shelf today. The old medicine shows never really went away, but took another form. Now television floods the room with shows, and then the huckster comes on selling a product. The advantage now is that we can just turn off the set. The medicine show did have an air of excitement about it and did cause a stir in the community. We, as kids, were always delighted when the show came to town.

At that time, even as today, psycho somatic illnesses exist, and there must have been some people helped by the "medicine" being sold simply by "auto suggestion." Well established sources indicate to us that 92% of illnesses are from improper attitudes, and this creates a negativism in us that disrupts our normal bodily functions. I may suggest that the investigative remedy for better health is to trust in the one who made you, and the health will improve dramatically if you follow His way.

ROLLING CIGARETTES

Kids from generation to generation are basically the same. Being of little means, we still like to imitate the adults, and one of the things we saw grown-ups do was smoke. We would get the corn silk from the top of the sweet corn, the brown stuff, and roll it in paper from a roll your own cigarette combination. That combination consisted of a small white bag of tobacco and cigarette paper. One of the leading sellers at that time was called Bull Durham.

We would borrow a paper or two and roll the corn silk in this. When it was not available, we rolled up dry apple leaves and tried that. This was all nonsense since we had no need for it and the taste was horrible anyway. Then too, it created a problem of smell, and we would have to scrub up real good before we got home so we wouldn't get caught. There was guilt involved; just sneaking into the house and avoiding your mother and father caused uneasiness.

SOFTBALL

As I grew older, sports occupied a lot of my time. I was playing a great deal of baseball and some soccer. Whereas we had street teams organized, there was structured baseball as well, which took the form of sandlot baseball. There were leagues in softball too, but my preference was handball. In softball, there were two sizes of balls. Twelve-inches and fourteen-inches. Fourteen-inch ball made a pretty big ball and slowed the game down considerably. This game prevailed for a limited time and lost its popularity. The 12" ball was lively and traveled further and made for a more exciting sport. It has survived to this day, but the format has been changed drastically.

There was a fast pitch 12" softball, and some pitchers were so adept at throwing the ball that at times it appeared they were throwing darts. The results were very low scoring games and very few hits. Apparently, pitchers' battles have gone out of style since the game has changed to the blooper ball. I accept that and even enjoy that type of ball, so I will be a spectator and those contests too when the occasion presents itself.

I found out too that softball was a means to picking up some extra cash since I had a job as a professional scorekeeper. You had to know the symbols for the score and play by play had to record it as the game went on. All players had a number associated with them, and certain events in the game were represented by a symbol. Just for example, if there was a strikeout, you put in the letter K.

At the age of fifteen, I went out for my first try-out in sandlot baseball. The classifications were F, E, D, C, and A. The "F" classification represented the initial basic starting point. Then you moved up to Class "E" and so forth according to your ability. Class "E" usually embraced the age bracket of sixteen and "D" between 16 and 18. You can gather from this that I had some audacity about myself since I shunned "F" and "E" and went out for try-out with a class "D" team at the age of FIFTEEN and *WAS ACCEPTED!* I must admit that I always had a lot of confidence in myself, and this was to prevail through the years: for many years, not only in sports but in other areas of my life as well.

I'll admit that many people would have thought I was cocky, but really, it was never meant to seem that way. Now, this attitude must have been very strong, since then I skipped class "C" and "B" and ended up playing "A" ball in the Akron sandlot! The way this came about was that I was familiar with the area of Bath, Richfield, and Peninsula. (Editor's note: that's where most of my mother's family lived) I was a frequent visitor to that area since my Uncle Stanley Scionka had a summer farmhouse out there and many of my summers were spent out there. This is how I became familiar with that surrounding locality. My cousins lived in that area (Balinskis, Scionkas) so there was plenty of opportunities to visit.

Apr 13, 1986. It so happened that I was out to visit the Balinskis around Richfield, Ohio. Leo, one of my cousins, said he was going out to the baseball field in Richfield to try out for a hardball team, class "A." Since he asked me to come along, we went together. They had a team pretty well established with just a few openings. As I watched the work-outs, I thought it would be nice to play for this team. It was then that I approached the manager and said I would like to try out. He asked what position I played, and my answer was that I played first base and pitched. He said that I could try out for pitcher since someone had taken first base.

I countered with the observation that if I were a manager, I would want the very best man for each position, and if anyone said they played a certain position, I'd at least give them a tryout. This way, I would know whether I had the best man or not. The manager then told me to go to first base and try out. They threw balls to me that were high and low and what not and hit ground balls of every description. I was "on" that day and didn't miss anything and ended up with the job. I also pitched when we needed a pitcher. This is the year that my batting average was a 500. To clarify at a certain point; I had some talent, but not that much. It happened that things worked well that year, and it seemed that everything fell into place. These last comments are not a shot at any false humility either; I'm just telling it as it was.

SPORTS

I played baseball in the army, too, both softball and hardball, but I shall go into further detail when I categorize my army days. In my early teens, we hung around the corner and did a lot of talking about sports. We had the Cleveland *Rams* for football, the Cleveland Indians for baseball, and the Cleveland Barons for Hockey. These were items of interest we discussed. The mention of the Rams is the same franchise that was moved to Los Angeles and is still there to this writing (1986). The Barons were not National League Hockey, but a step below (1930's). Never the less, they were a good team and would beat some of the National League teams.

They were very popular in Cleveland and drew crowds in the *twenty thousands* with consistency. (facility built to 10,000 capacity) Their home stadium was the Cleveland Arena, which was located at 37th and Euclid Avenue and closed in 1974 and was torn down. Paradoxically, I was not a hockey fan and only went to one game in my LIFE and walked out in the middle of it.

Pretty regularly on the weekend, we would have an outdoor dice game. The game was located right at the very end of Brow Avenue. There was good reason for this since gambling was illegal, and the police car made a regular patrol, which kept us on the alert. The game's location assured us a means of escape, when we saw the police car bearing down on us, we would head for the ravine, knowing that the cop would not chase us there. In the game itself, the stakes rose pretty high, and there was always a big winner. What I didn't like about it was that the game always had a big sore loser with the usual griping.

HOMEMADE ROOT BEER

We used to go into the valley and pick sassafras root. We would find a tree that, of course, was a sassafras tree, and it had to be a young tree so we could handle it. Grasping it as the trunk at the point nearest the root, we would pull and twist until the tree was uprooted. The root is the source of the flavorful juice of sassafras. This juice was important to us since we didn't buy more pop because of the expense, and sassafras had a taste that suggested Root Beer. Root Beer was my favorite drink, with ginger ale coming in second.

Speaking of Root Beer, Hires made an extract of Root Beer that could be purchased at the store. It came in a small bottle but was very concentrated and mixed with water with some yeast added; it was then put into bottles to age. The characteristic of home-made root beer was that the bottle always had the tell-tale deposit of yeast on the bottom. When opening and pouring, it was important to handle the bottle very carefully and not to stir up this creamy white substance. We became very good at it. The taste was excellent because there were many natural ingredients in the beverage. Today, deplorably, there are too many short-cuts to commercialism, inducing the manufacturer to rely on artificial ingredients as a by-product of being cost-conscious.

INGENUITY

On the corner of E. 52nd and Harvard Avenue, and directly across from E. 52nd was the Chef Boy Ardi (pizza) main factory. It was located right on the hill, just before it dipped into a deep valley and then back up again to the Newburgh Hts. Town Hall. Down in this valley was a flat piece of land, and when the torrential rains came, it flooded this valley and caused a little lake to form.

They dumped in that area too, and someone had thrown a flat piece of metal away that had sides about a foot high. It could have been about five feet square with no holes in it. So I dragged it over to the water and made a boat out of it. I would have a stick in the water that I pushed myself along with, and it was fun, but somehow, I lost five dimes that I had in my pocket. I never forgot it.

TRANSITION

Just about all of the narration thus far has dealt with my early youth, unless otherwise specified. Since my mind is just about searched out of the days of my youth, the next chapters will deal with my early teens and late teens. If anything of interest or importance comes to mind of my early youth, I will simply relate it and specify it as such.

As I entered my teens, the nonsense in my life seemed to lessen in proportion to my age. As previously noted, I was stupid to be on top of a six-story condemned building with a shaky ladder. Furthermore, my stupidity was amplified in challenging the police "to come and get us." We got hungry and tired and came down ourselves, and they promptly put us in jail. The police notified my parents to come and get me, and I was never so mortified in my life as at that time.

Now I have a better sense, but still hang around with the boys because in all the neighborhoods the groups were called gangs, and every neighborhood gang was opposed to other neighborhood gangs. There used to be fights between neighborhoods, but I started to avoid that or anything else that looked like trouble. When this happened, I just went home.

UNFORGETTABLE INCIDENTS

Two incidents affected me in my early teens that left a mark that lasts a lifetime. These two deal again with fear, but a compounded fear that goes over and above normal fear. The first incident involved the water. As I mentioned previously, all of my cousins lived on farms, and my visits there were frequent since my parents did a lot of visiting, and I went along. We went to Aunt Tillie's farm on this day, a farm with considerable acreage with cows, sheep, and some crops. Set off and away from the house was a home-made pool, not very large, but adequate for our needs of wading or swimming.

There were a number of us at the pool; one of them was Joe Witkowski, my sister Tillie's husband. He had been in and out of the pool, living it up, when he said to me, "Come on in, and I'll carry you on my shoulders!" I was hesitant at first, but he assured me that it would be alright. Trustingly, I got on his shoulders, he walked straight ahead and kept walking until he was submerged. He kept going down and down until I was entirely under the water! I was so surprised that I didn't even close my eyes as this murky water engulfed me. Everything looked tan before me as the water seemed to glare back at me.

Right at this time, I had nothing going for me, I didn't swim well, and Joe W. had such a grip on me that I couldn't shake loose. The full realization overwhelmed me in a wave of panic since, by now, my lungs were bursting for air. I kicked myself loose and surfaced. From there, whatever little knowledge I had of swimming was utilized fully and made it to shore in panic time. I told Joe off in no uncertain terms, but he drank a lot, and I doubt whatever I said would penetrate the alcohol barrier. This incident gave me an abnormal fear of water, which is difficult to overcome.

71

Every person is endowed with usual fears as a protective device. Still, when they are stretched beyond their bounds, the subconscious never lets go. It plays back the fears that are simulated in similar situations. This is truly an injustice since this causes limitations in a person's cope in life, plus the discomfort caused when encountering relevant situations.

Adding to this fear, a few years later was another situation that caused me a great deal of agony and consternation. My brother Walter and I went to the lakeshore one afternoon. It was Lake Erie, to be more specific. I may have cajoled him into taking me there since I recall nagging him to take me out on the lake in a rowboat. He wasn't responding to my nagging, and I persisted to the point that he may have become irritated. Then the eventful moment came, he got the boat and said, "Let's go." We rowed out very far, and now, being very far from land, he started to rock the boat vigorously to the point of being perilous. This rocking triggered another fear, coupled with the other water-related fear, and now I have another problem.

The treatment for this supposedly is to go out and do it again and again. I have done this in the past with some alleviation of the problem, but there is a segment that refuses to be eradicated. This is just a factual presentation of experience and feelings and not a solicitation of analysis or sympathy. I managed to survive in spite of this and participated in a war with plenty of boat rides and even swam in the Mediterranean Sea.

BALINSKI COUSINS

While relating the above incidents, two other incidents came to mind which should be appropriate to write here. The Balinski farm was visited often. This is the Walter and Tillie Balinski farm, and I differentiate because there was also a Frank and Nettie Balinski farm. Frank and Walter Balinski were brothers that married two sisters, Nettie (Anastasia) and Tillie Sobecki. They were sisters to my mother, Sophie.

Tillie and Walter had a family of all boys (six). Here they are in order of age Caesar, Gregory, Stephen, Leo, Raymond, and Richard. Nettie (the other Balinski wife) had four children: Chester and Leonard were the boys, and Agnes and Florence were the girls, and they lived on a private road in Peninsula, just north of route 303. We were usually at Tillie's farm and rarely at Nettie's, since to me, Nettie always seemed very ethnic and narrow. I don't know about my mother and father's sentiments, but it appeared their visits were limited on the Nettie Balinski side.

My relationship with the Balinski boys was close, especially to the boys of my age: Ray, Steve, Rich, and Leo. Greg and Caesar were older, and we were friends, but never had the common denominator of the compatible age similarities. The boys I would go swimming, play basketball, play cards, just house around. One time we were about to go somewhere for a ride in their pick-up truck. One of the boys mentioned that their dad, Walter Balinski, made his ow3n apple cider. I was about 13 (1933) at the time and unfamiliar with any potent libation pertaining to me. I had seen drinking and what it does to a person and had gained an adverse opinion toward it.

Now this situation was different, I realized. These are my cousins and were out to have a good time – and why not? The barrel of cider was in a lower alcove of the house just adjacent to the basement. We all had a cupful or less, I can't remember exactly, but I remember it tasted sooo good and in a short time made me feel equally mellow. It was an experience that lasts to this day.

Another time, I was at their farm (Tillie & Walter Balinski), and my mother permitted me to stay overnight. (Remember Frank's parents lived in the city-Marcia) Brothers Rich and Stan Scionka were there too. They are my cousins. We talked Aunt Tillie into letting us sleep in the hay barn that night. The contingent about to partake in this adventure was Rich and Stan and the three younger Balinski brothers – Steve, Ray, Rich, and then myself. Their German shepherd also accompanied us, and I was very impressed with him because he could climb a ladder straight up.

We went out to the barn with a lot of boyish enthusiasm and the spirit of adventure, never realizing that there was more adventure in store for us than we bargained for. We all climbed the ladder to the first loft of hay, and there was another loft above. We had brought along a feather comforter or a "piezinia" we called it. We bedded down, and there was the usual amount of horsing around and chatter which lasted a long time, but we began to dwindle as we got sleepier, warm, cozy, and relaxed.

Finally, we said the last good night, and we drifted off to sleep. Shortly after, one of the boys said, "stop throwing that hay on me and go to sleep." The other boy swore religiously that he didn't do it. A few times, the accusations and denials happened. The denials were so emphatic now that it became evident that the hay throwing was coming from the *upper* loft from some *uninvited* company. We decided to vacate the barn, and there was no conference or consultation necessary. The decision was instantaneous and concise, without a doubt! When we got outside of the barn (still dark outside), we gathered some rocks and threw them up into the direction of the upper hayloft.

Suddenly, we heard a noise emanating from the upper hayloft, and we took off like the Indy 500. It was very funny in retrospect since Rich Scionka, who was holding this big feather piezinia, ran with it and passed us all by on the way to the house about a hundred and fifty feet away. The next morning, Greg, the older brother (who wasn't part of the barn crowd) would never let us forget how cowardly we were and said we should have called HIM to investigate. Well, it was a lot of fun and an experience to remember.

Greg, Leo, Steve, and Ray all played musical instruments, and they put this to good use and organized a band. Greg played the saxophone, Steve the trumpet, Ray on the drums, and Leo on the clarinet. They made good music and played for dances that I attended as often as I could, but it was mainly to meet girls and not to hear their music. These were very enjoyable times, and we did a lot of friendly fooling around had had a closeness that had a lot of warmth. For instance, very often, we would get together at different homes for poker games. These Balinski boys were very normal since you could see they were close, but they fought among themselves all the time about something or other.

We played for money and sometimes all night long, but after the first time, I skipped the all-night routine since it lost some of its glamour as the wee hours built up. In basketball, which was played in the hay barn, it was everything goes with no holds barred. There was a lot of cheating and unsportsmanlike conduct exercised here, and everyone accepted it as normal, and I suppose it was. It was common to steal the ball out of a guy's hands and even wrestle him to the floor to get it.

RACCOON HUNTING

The next episode with the Balinskis occurred in the wintertime when we all decided we should go raccoon hunting bare-handed. Fresh snow that had just fallen, about two inches of it, an unblemished white blanket spreading throughout the woods. The object was to identify the animals' tracks and simply follow him to where he went. This plan worked fine since it wasn't too long that we saw a coon's tracks and started to track it. Now, if you have any sanity about you at all, wild raccoons are not the prime animal to catch, especially with bare hands. They can claw and bite and cause a lot of physical damage that could be fatal, not to mention rabies or some other infections. We never discussed that as we followed the hot trail to a hollow log.

There no tracks leading out of the log, so we knew the coon was in there! Hearts beat faster, and the coursing blood took turns running hot and cold. It was a little odd breaking a sweat in that cold air, but it was in the spirit of the occasion. Now that we located the coon, it remained the task to get him out. The method we employed was to get a limb with flexible branches, push it into the hollow log, and start to twist. This method would cause the small branches to become entangled in the coon's hair and attach sufficiently enough to pull him out.

Of course, we realized that the raccoon would become frightened and hostile, bristling mad, and would be exhibiting his objections when we pulled him out. It was vital to neutralize his hostility, we accomplished this by throwing a very heavy garment over him at the point of exit. The timing had to be perfect since he could have broken loose and attacked or made off with a good coat (ours).

One of my Balinski cousins punched him and held on firmly while there was a raging inferno going on inside the coat. It was determined that the coon should be taken home to the Balinski residence/farm and placed in a suitable safe place. Our long-range plans did not answer the question: why we wanted a wild raccoon in the first place?

We arrived at the Balinski residence and deposited the frenzied animal in the upstairs bathroom, making sure we locked the door rapidly. No one was interested in dealing with the coon and any of his spontaneous plans.

Shortly after that, Aunt Tillie arrived on the scene, and there was some apprehension on our part as to how she would receive this news. That was not exactly your commonplace everyday happening. The reader of this story should ask himself how often he or she has experienced such a thing. To my recollection, her response was not panicky or one of great alarm. There was some surprise in her reaction, but an indication that she had unusual experiences in the past and was getting to be a veteran at this sort of thing. Her instructions minced no words when she told us to get the animal out of the house.

We had no set plans as to how to do this, for no one had projected that far ahead, but we reasoned that the 'coon had a plan, and we let him carry it out. We simply opened the door to the bathroom, left all the other doors open as well, and we stood aside. The coon found daylight faster than a rooster catching the first glimpse of the sun – and he was gone! That was the first and last time I ever did that, but that one time was more than sufficient.

BEST FRIEND

My association with the Balinskis was close and amicable usually, but there is always someone has as a close friend or a best friend, and I was no exception to that rule. My best friend was my cousin Richard, brother of Stanley, their sister, Della (Adele), whose parents were Stanley and Francis Scionka. Richard's personality was low-key, and his sense of humor would match mine. In other words, we were compatible and got along fine, and spent some fine years together. Richard played the piano as well as his brother, Stan. But Stan played in an improvised manner and had some inventiveness about him. Rich played by the book almost blandly. This, however, is just an observation and certainly wasn't meant to mean anything else.

Rich and I spent the most time together at his home and at his father's summer farm-home. I recall one thing we did together that proves, once and for all, that if you don't know how to do something, don't do it. One evening we were home alone, and we were talking about cream puffs and how much we liked them. Suddenly the idea light went on, and we embarked on this adventure of trying to make cream puffs. We had a recipe, but definitely, no expertise and the way the dough went into the oven is exactly the way it came out – only baked and kind of black. Years later, when I had my bakery,

I learned how to make cream puffs the right way.

Rich took a course in horticulture in high school, East Tech specifically, and their classes originated at a place called Harvey Rice Gardens located on E. 116th off Miles or Union. He was always interested in growing plants and trees. This interest fit well into the continuity of his father's plans, since Uncle Stanley was prone to horticulture too.

Uncle Stanley Scionka Sr., Rich's father, was without reservation one of the finest men I have ever met in my life. He was intelligent and kind, generous and slow to anger, and very understanding and warmly reserved. We would make many trips to the country with Uncle Stanley and work with him at his hobby. Interestingly, working with him was fun, and he had my deep respect and admiration. We would plant new evergreen trees and tend to his dahlias, of which he had myriads of varieties. This flower is very beautiful but not very hardy and does not last long as a cut plant.

In the fall, all of the bulbs had to be dug out and put in a secure place protecting them from freezing. If not, they perished very easily. Even today, that area is a testimonial to Uncle Stan and his work since the pine trees still flourish as silent witnesses. There was a lot of time spent out on this farm, and I will spin off into some of the things we did. During the summer, it was not uncommon for the parents to allow us to stay on the farm by ourselves for a few nights at a time. The house was a bungalow style but was unfinished inside. The walls were lathed and awaited the plaster that never came. This was immaterial to us, for a young man's fancy turns to other things other than interior decorating.

FARM

The home acted as a good jumping-off place to other activities that existed in Peninsula, Ohio. There, quite frequently, were outdoor movies and girls. There also were dances and girls. It was also a town with a few stores, and some activity, which alleviated some of the loneliness of prolonged stays on the farm.

Close to the house, outside were two sugar pear trees that had really delicious pears that make my gastric juices flow even now as I think of it. As you would face the front of the house, a makeshift drive was to the left of it, the pear trees were to the left of the house, and in the back and to the left was a big tall willow tree, followed by a small pond or lake about 22 feet across and 30 feet wide that was spring fed. Right behind the pond was a scrumptious Bartlett pear tree. These pears, too, were simply delicious, and we had our fill and never tired of them.

Going toward the back were rows of pine trees Uncle Stan had planted and had grown to about fifteen feet high by this time. We could go inside the trees that had grown close together, and it was like a recluse of some sort. The sun would filter through the needles, with a soft muted glow, and the needles that had fallen in years past formed a soft carpet-like surface that lent a spring to the step. The scent of the trees, with their distinctive and unique pleasantness, added to this sanctuary of serenity.

When the season was right, some mushrooms sprouted in this area, and we delighted my uncle by picking them and presenting them to him. Going back, was fifty-seven sprawling acres that we roamed, some parts being rolling fields and other parts densely wooded. There was some poison ivy, which we at times crashed through with an abandon, Stan used to catch it, but I seemed to have an immunity to it.

One morning Stan woke up with an unusual amount of vigor. We were both in bed with our clothes on; he challenged me to a dash to the pond and an instant bath. He coaxed me into doing this, but much probing wasn't needed. It was summer, but the mornings always were cool, yet this hardly could be constructed as a deterrent. Almost as if there were a fixed command, we jumped up, dashed to the back of the house, out the kitchen door, and to the left where the pond lay with cool, open arms. At TOP speed, we streaked to the pond, and at its bank, two human forms were catapulting through space for the short period that it took to make contact with the spring-fed invigorating waters.

The splash was tremendous, the instant wake-up total, the saturation complete from head to toe. This incident was positively exhilarating, the rapid gasping for breath as the chilly temperatures of the frigid water plunged body temperatures rapidly downward. Needless to say, our stay was short, and the departure was instant. Stan discovered, to his dismay, that he had jumped into the pond with a full pack of cigarettes in his pocket.

There used to be a commercial for Camel cigarettes that said, "I'd walk a mile for a Camel." We must have walked twenty miles at least for a Lucky

Strike! (Another brand of cigarettes). These are factual reports and do not in any way advocate the use of cigarettes for anyone. These are the things that I did, neither condemning these things or inducing anyone to follow this path. Whoever realizes, should know that to profit from someone else's experience, good or bad, is to add to the quality of your LIFE which I desire for all. Yet, I must relate all types of incidents in the vein of honesty for you to get a concerted picture of who I was and what I have become. We are incomplete human beings that, after being exposed to life and its lessons, should become more mature, more complete, more responsible, and therefore, take a useful place in society to contribute to the world and its betterment. The most deplorable thing to see is a person staying useless and just occupying space. This is a drag on society and a detriment as well.

BITTERSWEET VINES

Now that a description has been given of the farm and no doubt remains vague in your concept, I should like to relate an adventure that resulted in lucrative aspects. Out in the rolling acres and the wooded areas grew a plant called bittersweet. It is a creeping vine that winds and wends its way in all directions, engulfing anything in its path. In the fall, it produces a berry with a green exterior pod about the size of a lima bean but perfectly round.

We would cut the vines to make bouquets, making sure to get the vines with the healthiest and most abundant berries. When we collected them in quantity, they were taken to the farmhouse and made up into bunches. These bunches then were hung upside down to dry, and this caused the berries to burst open. The green shell would open into four segments and reveal a beautiful flaming red berry within. This, in contrast to the open pod, lent dramatic color to the array. After all the assembly, we would carefully pack the bouquets and drive up to route 21, where a makeshift stand was installed, and the bittersweet was put on display. The compacted bunches of bittersweets, with their fiery inflamed hues of flamingo and oranges, were further enhanced by the intense sunlight lending a captivating brilliance.

Passing cars would stop, and drivers would inquire as to the nature of the plant and its usage. We would enlighten the potential customer with a brief history of the plant and emphasized that the most distinguished homes have displayed bittersweets for years throughout the long dreary winter. We would remind them that the plant lasts all winter and maintains its fiery brilliance through the dark, drab days, with cheerful, eye-catching colors. We sold a lot of bittersweets and made a handsome profit.

MAKE-SHIFT RADIO

In these days, television was just an idea in the inventor's mind, and we just heard suggestions that someday television would be possible. We relied on radio, and to us, this was sufficient. The radio had developed rapidly, but there were no small portable radios or other sophisticated electronic gadgets. They simply had not been invented yet. We would have a contraption of the simplest nature that would get one station. Even that was not easy, since there was a thin wire that had to make a contact with a silvery looking stone we called a magneto (provides current).

We would select certain spots until the right contact was made and receptions was received. When we heard sound through the headphones, we were delighted. Now magneto means electric force mainly generated by magnetism, and the stone acted as a magnet and could act as its own generator. There is an iron ore product called magnetite, which is strongly attracted by a magnet, and even acts as a magnet itself and its common name is loadstone. This proper contact plays an important part in creating ignition. Of course, as kids, we didn't know this; we knew it was an important part of our "crystal set," which in reality was a basic radio.

In the farm area was a radio station located on Route 21 that had the call letters WTAM. This radio station was so powerful that we accidentally discovered that by putting our ear to certain downspouts on the back of the house, we could hear that station at times! My cousin Leonard, a son of the other Balinski clan (Anastasia Sobecki/Balinski was his mother), took the crystal set a step further and connected a loudspeaker to it. Everyone in the room could hear it then, and the system with the speaker looked very much like RCA's emblem with the dog on the speaker.

NASH CAR

My Uncle Stanley had a Nash car made by American Motors. It was a beautiful car, but he seemed to have motor trouble with it, and often, it would not run. The times it did run, though, we went out on old route 21 out to the farm. (Boston Mills Road off of Black Road/Richfield Twp) Route 21 at that time was just a two-lane road, but there was no need for anymore since cars weren't in abundance. I recall roaring down the road at a top speed of forty miles an hour, and we were all very impressed. This reminds me of my very first ride in an automobile, I experienced car sickness and had to throw-up. There was another time when I was very small that I rode in an old model that was open on the sides, and when a storm came up, we had to snap on plastic curtains.

Getting back to Uncle Stan and the Nash, though, I recall one trip out the country that was very eventful! The main roads were adequate since they were basically built from baked red brick, which we still see today when a blacktop piece breaks away, and the red brick is exposed. The country roads were just roads that were formed by the horse and wagon. After much wear, they were very dusty in a dry climate, and very muddy after a rain. Large holes would also develop. When a farmer got stuck, he urged the horses to use extra effort to get out. These were "roads" available to us to get to the farm.

So, on our way to the farm, we turned down this dirt road, which was very muddy, for it must have rained recently. We went along slowly, but not slow enough not to get stuck. Suddenly, the car hit a deep muddy spot in the road and went out of control. The next thing we knew, the car turned over, and we were laying our side. No one got hurt; Rich, Stan, and I had to take a walk up the road to Uncle Walter's house and solicit help. He hitched up the team of horses and up righted us and pulled us out of the ditch. He got a laugh out of this, and for a long time, when people had troubles with their cars, the expression "get a horse" was very popular.

FAMILY NEXT DOOR

Still, in my early teens, I must relate this segment of my home life since my neighbors play a part in my development to adulthood. Next to us lived a family named Podojil, and they had a girl and two boys. The boys and girl were older than me, yet they liked me very much, and I spent time with them, and their mother would give me little treats on occasion. The boys were John and Eddie, and their sister was Lily. She was a nice-looking lady, and even at my tender age, I noticed. Ed and John took to me as to a younger brother, and they were always asking my mother's permission to take me either to a movie or a sporting event or fishing, etc. They would give a football game a particular buildup by telling me, guys get hurt sometimes and get carried off the field on stretchers. This bit of news seemed to be fascinating, and everyone seemed to find satisfaction in that. This fascination is just another aspect of the young male mentality or lack of thereof. This is why I realize the importance of tolerance for young people and the things they do that are asinine since I did many things that came out stupid to me now.

Mrs. Podojil was a real nice lady, and I remember her as being kind and considerate. She and my mother would spend a lot of time by the fence "holding it up" as the conversation went on and on. Mr. Podojil was really a separate entity; I realized he was a good man, even when he scared me with his booming voice and rugged appearance. It seemed to me that Mr. Podojil was a big beer drinker, but this may be a misconception on my part. I drew this conclusion from the fact that I was his favorite chaser.

To elucidate: At that time, most beers were draft beers, and Mr. Podojil had a system that worked like a charm. He had a little tin bucket, shiny and bright, with a handle on it that must have held either a pint or a quart. When he wanted a beer, you could hear his gruff low voice, loaded with volume and a carrying capacity that must have had its own call letters and frequency! Wherever I was, the word "FRANKIE" would come tumbling through the air in an authoritative, demanding command, and I dropped everything and came running. There was a little tip in it, and that's why I came running since I knew he would sweeten the pot.

I'd take the bucket and go skipping off to the beer palace on the corner of E. 55th and Brow, Novak's Tavern. The bartender would fill the bucket, and sometimes I would forget I had the beer and would skip off with beer splashing off the sides of the can. Mr. Podojil *always reminded me* that some beer was missing and that I should exercise a lot of care. It is really tough not to spill a drop or two. May God's blessings be on the Podojils!

MY MOTHER, SOPHIA SOBECKI TRASKA

Let me tell you about my mother and her great love for flowers. We had a rather large backyard, and usually, people would plant grass in such a large area. Mother, saw it a little differently, however. She had a portion set off for a vegetable garden, but its size compared to her flower garden left no room for doubt, which was her preference. The yard was filled with many varieties of flowers, and it was a pleasure to see the variety of colors. The scent was enjoyable as a summer breeze carried it gently to the nostrils of any passerby.

Growing from the back porch was a vigorous, hardy vine of morning glories, that when in bloom, burst onto the scene with magnificent splendor, singing a symphony in blue and white. Mother had grape vines too, and she gave me some cuttings, which I planted in my backyard and still grow to this day. She included some morning glory seeds as well, and they too grew very well. At this time, they are threatening to take over my whole yard, front, and back. God bless mother!

As you recall, I mentioned going to church at eight years old and hearing a priest say, "love God with your whole heart and your whole soul." These words were a seed that started to take root in my young mind. The seed would slowly grow until at about eighteen years of age, the curiosity started to demand that I should investigate what this is all about. Up until this point, and through habit, I would attend Mass to satisfy my mother. Consequently, my attendance was purely methodical and systematic with no gain for myself whatever.

FINDING RELIGION

I recall very clearly going to church, meeting some of the boys, and then spending time with them on the outside, biding my time until Mass was over. When I came home, my mother would ask if I went to church, and I would answer, "Yes, I went to the church." Phonetically this was correct, but it certainly wasn't what she meant. Yet, these are some of the games we play. The awakening happened on this one summer day at age eighteen or so. Standing across the street from St. John Nepomucene, and just before I was to cross and enter the church, I asked myself, "Why am I doing this? What's this all about?"

I went into the church, but from that point on, I was resolved to find out what this religion was all about. There was a decision to be made; either I would embrace it or reject it. In fairness, I knew that I should look into all segments of worship. This decision should include all branches of the

Protestants, Hindu, Mohammedism, Buddhism, Christian Science, and Jehovah's Witness. Now, I may not have listed them all, but believe me, I touched on them all. Through all this research, an interesting fact emerged that impressed me right to my very core.

I read that up until the year 1490; there was no other Christian church except the Catholic church. This fact was very impressive to me; here was a church established for one thousand and five hundred years and still in existence. The Protestant branches were only a mere four hundred years old, yet here was a church 1500 years old, still standing and growing. It occurred to me that had this church not existed; the Protestants would have nothing to branch off of.

The Catholic Church's oneness is impressive, too, since the same Mass is celebrated in the same way, regardless of nationality or country. Studying further, I discovered that the Protestant church had, by this time and from its beginning, branched out into 400 different type churches—each disagreeing in some aspect, sufficient to divide them into various worship categories. I couldn't see any oneness there, and I perceived humanness in these separations, not Divine guidance.

Do not regard this dissertation as a criticism of other forms of worship; however, the conclusions I arrived at fit me and my make-up, and suit me, so I can live with it, accept it, embrace it, and dedicate myself to it. This, I feel, is what God wants of me, to be able to put myself to His purpose honestly and faithfully with all of me participating. The avenue he opened to me is the Catholic church, and since God is a God of variety, He may have many other avenues or channels He uses. On my part, this is speculation and my human opinion, and no narrowness of mind should be attributed to me over this.

Certainly, whatever you believe honestly leads you to God's love and His Kingdom would be the right course for you. I hope that I have established that my concerted efforts are toward being unbiased, which demands an open mind and God's revelation. At any rate, at eighteen years of age, I have my initial beginning. Henceforth, God will interact in my life and I with Him. It is a prolonged process as the Lord reveals slowly to mold the person who sincerely seeks Him.

Back to the eighteen years of age and the neophyte Christian who had made a decision and wasn't even aware of it, but God was. There always was an interest in me about Jesus, and in my early years, I wondered if He ever lived at all and were all figments of someone's imagination. I would look at a crucifix and see Christ hanging there and would think, "you have to be a sucker to do that." This was all in the formulation process, due to my gross ignorance of anything religious and my unwillingness to learn anyway. I credit this to my introduction to Christianity, which wasn't presented most kindly or positively. Yet, if there is truth in any person, the Good Lord will cause it to grow.

Now that I am on a course of being a Catholic, I am able to listen a little more in church. Just a little more, and there were many, many Masses that I couldn't wait until they were over. Yet, in spite of myself, some of the readings and Gospel had to rub off.

MIDDLE AND HIGH SCHOOL

The incidents I have been relating all happened in my early years. When I started going to high school, I had more sense. I still hung around with the gang, but when it looked like they were going to get into trouble, I went home. I was about sixteen or so at that time.

Life at Fowler Junior High was pleasant enough, and I did not get into much trouble there. It was there that I had my first revelation that maybe I did have some brains after all. The subjects in school were the standard subjects that all schools have. One was Algebra and awful sounding name at the time. The name suggested to me the most awful of connotations. Yet, it wasn't as bad as all that. As I listened in class, the teacher explained it, and I understood. What shocked me was the number of students who didn't. They kept looking around for someone who understood, and I said that I did. So, they had me explaining the lessons to them in between classes and after school. This was my first positive introduction to some self-confidence, an increase in my self-worth, and a feeling that maybe I wasn't so dumb after all. This moment equates to the fact that children should be encouraged and complimented for their accomplishments. Above all, no one should push them beyond their limitations. I believe someone can cause severe damage to a child by insisting that they are capable of doing something they cannot do. On the other hand, encouragement and love will help them want to do their best without frustration. At times would be difficult to arrive at because of our humanity, but no rule says we can't grow with the child.

At Fowler, we had gym classes, which I liked because the activity appealed to me. One activity they had was boxing, and this was whole class participation. As we partook in this so-called manly self-defense, I was pleasantly surprised by the instructor when he asked me where I had learned to fight. Instead of making me a pupil, he made me an instructor for the other kids. This was a good boost for my ego and self-worth. They also had regular boxing matches throughout the school year; this was optional if you wished to join or not. I joined and did rather well, won my preliminary bouts, but lost to a kid named Pironni on points. It happened that his brother was a professional heavyweight, and Joe, the kid I fought, trained with his brother Patsi. This kid was well trained, and I was aware of it as I lost on points. It is also apparent that with all this knowledge, I got psyched out. In other words, pretty scared, but I fought him anyway. Second-best isn't that bad anyway.

Fighting to me wasn't anything new since there was a lot of that in our neighborhood and in the surrounding area. We were all in depressed areas, as they are referred to today. The kids were generally kids of ethnic people, and the economy wasn't that good at that time. We all had to scrape for a living. I will elaborate further on this in future chapters. At Fowler Junior High, I managed to be a good boy and didn't get into any trouble. There was one incident, though, that I had to resolve because it annoyed me very much, and I thought it had gone too far and too long. Every school will have its hotshot, and this school was no exception. This kid's name was Kovach, and he always acted big and traveled with a couple of other kids. They were always smarting off. They thought they were God's gift to women and used different obnoxious ways to get attention.

One day Kovach and his crew ran into me on the second floor of the auditorium. They proceeded to pull that hotshot stuff on me. I told them I thought they were phony and asked if they would like to prove to me just how tough they really were. To make a long story short, I punched out Kovach, and his helpers didn't lend a hand. Things were better around the school after that. There was a black kid too that was pushing people around, so I took him on too. We never finished it at Fowler, but we met again at South High School. At South High, he learned to be more respectful. He was big, 6 foot 2 inches.

Please know, I am not trying to impress anyone that I was a tough guy. I am just trying to show that I stood for justice and my freedom. I resent being intimidated, and it annoyed me when someone tried to get away with that type of behavior. I was not a hoodlum, and I never went out of my way to find a fight. As a matter of fact, anytime I took someone on, there was always some fear connected to it. Yet, I felt that if this continued, it would only compound the situation, so it is necessary to act positively in certain situations.

My memories of the school are pleasant; I had a good friend whose name was Harry Moronski. He went by the name of Harry Moore. He was a boxer and won the golden gloves division of the welterweights. This is in the 160-pound class. This kid used to ask me to work out with him so we would box together. Whereas I fought him pretty well, I always felt that he could have done better if he tried. This is the first time I met anyone who could punch a punching bag like a professional with that rat-a-tat-tat. After all these workouts and training, I found out that he won the championship.

At South High School, I remember coming in as a tenth-grade flat. The tradition of looking down at a freshman was prevalent. I suppose this will continue for as long as there are schools and freshmen. In South High, I had friends, and we ran around together. One was Jerome Domanski, a self-made politician who continually played the angles. Another was Joe Dembowski, who was a lot of fun and whose dad owned a beer joint, which he inherited eventually. Maransky was another friend, but his last name escapes me. He was a straight-A student and a real egghead. We got along well, and it was on his encouragement that my grades really came up in high school.

There was an exclusive club in South High called the scroll and key. The primary requisite for being able to join was that you had to make the honor roll. The honor roll consisted of two A's in major subjects and nothing lower than a B in all the other subjects. Of course, there was no rule that you had to get B's to be on the honor roll. This was just the bare minimum. With this motivation, I got on the honor roll for three straight years and was in the scroll and key three straight years.

The other members voted for you to become a member. There was an initiation that was fun as well and being clever. One of the things you had to do was drink a glass of soapy water. They then sat you in a chair and blindfolded you. As you sat there blindfolded, they continued to talk among themselves as you listened. The conversation went like this. "No, don't put that red hot poker on his arm; you will burn him." Someone else would say, "Yes, but if he wants to be a member, it is worth a little burn, Isn't it?" As they bantered back and forth, they finally said 'Let's do it.' Just then, you felt this sensation on your arm, and you would swear it was hot. It was an ice cube. In the same vein, they said there was raw oyster that they would rub on my face and arms or any exposed part. It became very effective with proper hype, and for a few moments, it felt like it was a raw oyster. It was really a wet, cold tissue with a little soap to make it slippery. There were other gags that they pulled, but they escape me.

I was in a club called Mask and Wig. This club put on school plays in which I had parts, but just a couple. One was about the Japanese, and another was about Lincoln. Both parts were minor. One time, I had to address an auditorium full of people with a memorized speech. I just about blew it because I almost froze up there until a teacher assisted me. I was also a participant in a school guard program where you sat in the hall as a student guard and only permitted people whit a pass to go about their business. Of course, there was some fooling around in school, but I was lucky not to get caught too often. I did get caught smoking in the hallway once, but that was because of my stupidity and so-called daring. How slowly some of us learn. By and large, though, I wanted to stay free of trouble since I wanted to be on the baseball team and on the football team. Basketball never interested me, and I never tried out for it. Even today, basketball had no real fascination for me.

To be factual, my interest in basketball will arouse for special games. I always wish teams well that represent Cleveland. This would come under the category of civic pride. Lastly, I am not that narrow-minded that exceptional talent is not appreciated. Yet, it is deplorable when some exceptionally talented player has an inflated ego over a talent that was given by God. To pursue this thought one more step, which deals with the tremendous amount of money that these stars are making. I feel that any athlete is in a fantastic position to help the less fortunate by example and monetarily. These are my opinions, and I should have to question myself as to what I would do if I were blessed with an unusual talent and what my actions would be. I should like to think it would not change me but admit that the influence would be great. I occasionally runoff into an essay-type report, and they are my opinions.

At South High, I tried out for the Baseball team in my first year. This usually is a no-no, since a freshman is supposed to be relegated to the Junior Varsity. I aspired to get on the regular varsity, and I always felt confident that I could do that. I don't know where this confidence developed, but it was almost the point of cockiness. Yet, I did make the baseball team the first year and was a pitcher as a regular on the staff. You might say that I did have some raw talent, very raw, whereas there was some ability, the experience was lacking. Due to this, it was not uncommon for me to walk the bases loaded yet end up striking out the side without any runs being scored.

Now I didn't plan it that way. It just happened. When I think of that poor coach and manager who had to go through these uneasy moments, I have sympathy. Being able to make the team the first year brought out an unusual characteristic in me that I feel is a defect of character. When the challenge was met and overcome, I lost interest in being on the team and I believe I quit in my final year. This exhibited a lack of dedication and no doubt a selfish outlook. Yet being aware of something like that lets me have the occasion to change it. After all, any person who ever lives will find that real success in life is conquering oneself.

The football team was a little tougher to make because here again, I tried for the varsity. Football is full of big heavy guys, and the chances of tall, lean guys weighing in around 160 weren't that good. Yet, the game is played by desire and heart and the underlying selfish reason of wanting to be someone, especially in the girls' eyes in the school. High School football can be very grueling. The workouts are barbaric and taxing, but barring injury, they do put you in good shape physically. Mental toughness is an important factor in training in addition to the sacrifice and expenditure of your free time. I made the team despite my weight and won the position of right half back.

Not to create any illusions, I made the second team and was used sparingly. One time, I was in on the kick-off return team and returned the ball to the opposing team's 45-yard line. The tacklers didn't really bother me that much, yet no one really likes to get hit. I got hit by a bunch of them, as many as could get near me. This in itself was bearable, but when they piled on with me on the bottom, you have to idea what that is like. It is totally black under there with no air to breathe, and it seems like an eternity until the officials get them all off. That is the bad part, it was very scary.

My football days were shortened by the injury to my brother Pete. The injury he sustained playing street football that resulted in the tragedy that took his life. It was the end of my football days; my mother would no longer sign the approval paper allowing me to play. I remember being very bitter and disappointed at the time. But thank God for parents and their good sense and tenacity in sticking to a decision. Despite all my pleadings, the answer was still NO. As I reflect on that now, they could have saved me an injury that I could have carried the rest of my life.

At South High, a school of co-education, it is a normal to notice girls and for girls to notice boys. There was a girl that caught my eye, whose name was Dorothy Wysocky. In my sight, she had to be the most beautiful, delectable morsel that ever existed. It frightened me to even come near her; to just be in her presence made me nervous and very uneasy. This romance never got off the ground because you cannot function very well when you are petrified. There was some irony to this situation since Dorothy had a girlfriend named Jean Peters. Jean was tall, blond, very attractive, and was interested in me. She apparently was experiencing the same type of nervousness as I toward Dorothy.

My football coach, Mr. Unger, kept prodding me to date Jean. He said she was a real doll and was attracted to me. I told him to talk to Dorothy for me, but he kept saying that Jean was the best catch. I went with Jean for a short while, and then the whole deal fell apart. The puppy love wore off, and later I dated a girl with long black hair, slim and willowy. Things ended with her also, as I realized that I just wanted company but no serious attachments. That is enough of my romantic attachments in high school.

In those days, transportation was by a streetcar when it was feasible to do so. Transportation to South High was not possible due to a lack of funds. Apparently, the school was not considered too far since I used to walk it every day, rain or shine, blizzard or bitter cold. We really didn't think much of it since it was a way of life and a natural lifestyle. When I went to Fowler, I went by streetcar. I would catch the streetcar on the top of Harvard hill. Before the freeway went in, there was a big valley from 52nd St. up to the town hall, so the name Harvard Hill. I would walk each morning to the streetcar stop on Washington Park Blvd. My dog Archie would always escort me right to the town hall corner. Then I would tell him I had to leave, and he should go home. He always did.

Here is the story of how I got Archie. One very cold winter day, while it was getting on to evening, I heard a noise on my front porch. Looking out the front window, I saw this mongrel dog, hungry, shaking, alone, and abandoned. My mother made me aware in times past that whereas she liked dogs, she didn't want one in the house. Faced with this obstacle, there was nothing I could do except put a carpet on the porch for him to sleep and a little food because I was sure he was hungry. He ate the food and took a liking to the carpet, but the wind was so severe that it whipped the snow around in sharp blasts. It bothered me that the dog might freeze. After a while, I approached my mother and told her what was on my mind. "Please, mother, could I just put him in the garage where he will be out of the wind and snow!" My mother said yes, and from then on, it was only a matter of time that I got him into the house. We were good pals and went everywhere together. His name was inspired by a radio program called Duffy's Tavern.

The Radio program always opened with "Hello Duffy's Tavern. Duffy ain't in Archie speaking." Archie's voice was the typical bartender voice of days gone by, crude and unrefined but somehow pleasant and nonthreatening. It seemed to be a good name for my dog, and so it was. Archie and I spent a few years together, and then he began to have trouble with his eyes. Specifically, he was developing cataracts and of the most severe kind. It was very disheartening because he was starting to bump into things, and it was becoming more evident that I could not keep him. Medical treatment was impossible since we had hardly enough money to live, but nothing could mitigate the love I felt for my dog and his impending loss.

The Good Lord was mindful of a young boy's dilemma and placed it in my mind to ask my uncle Walter, who owned a farm, to give him a home on there. Walter was my mother's brother and lived on the farm with his brother John. Of course, I was apprehensive that no one would want a dog that was blind and therefore not much use. Uncle Walter was a real dog lover and had about ten fox terriers that he kept in a kennel built on his farm. He also had a couple of other dogs that just roamed around. When I asked if he would take the dog, my heart jumped with joy when he said yes. Now I would know how Archie was doing, and I know that Uncle Walter would take good care of him. Archie lived several years after that, and I was able to visit him from time to time. Thank God for compassionate people. I hope that I have covered my school days and things connected with them.

FIRST FULL-TIME JOB

Shortly after high school, I was thrown into the job market with countless other graduates. This in itself was deplorable since the job market virtually did not exist (1938/1939). These were very depressed times, and there weren't many jobs around. There were many experienced men out of work, and my chances of getting employed were less than theirs. Every place I went to seek employment simply gave me an application, as they did the countless others that applied, and filed me behind the others. The years in the 1930s were not good years and indeed were far from being prosperous.

It was common for people to be in debt and have mortgages on their homes, and there were many foreclosures. My mother and dad had a mortgage on our home through the government, a program called FHA or Federal Housing Admin. I am not sure if this was the correct name, but there was a program of low-interest mortgages run by the government. I hope that the picture is clearly drawn of conditions in that era, so you may fully understand the almost utter hopelessness of my getting a job.

My efforts to gain employment did not cease, but it was demoralizing. One day a scripture came into my mind, and it related to persistence. It was a story of a man banging on his neighbor's door in the middle of the night. The neighbor was in bed and refused to open the door, but the man kept pounding on the door until it was opened. There was another scripture about a woman before a judge, and this too dealt with persistence. In both cases, they wore the person down by persistently seeking their specific need and obtained it. This became the basis for my plan to get a job, after all, it worked for them, why not for me?

First, I picked out a place that I wanted to work, and that happened to be the Powerlite Switchboard Company on E. 78th and Harvard Avenue. My first call there was greeted by the usual format: filling out an application and the "we'll let you know" bit. The next day at 9:00 AM sharp, I was there again asking for a job. The man said or asked, "Weren't you here yesterday?" I said, "Yes, but there will be a job opening here someday, and I want to be the first one in line to get it." I planned to go there every day, day in and day out, and wear them down without being obnoxious. The Bible wrote about persistence, and this is what I intended to do. It got to the point that each morning at 9:00 AM, the foreman expected me, and seemed to like me, and the display of the persistent attitude.

About two weeks later, the foreman told me I had made my point, and I should save myself the trouble of coming every day. He gave me his assurance that the next job opening was mine. It was a Thursday, he called the next day, and Saturday was my first day of work. This was a tremendous day in my life because being broke for so long makes you helpless and feel desperate. The company manufactured switchboards for lighting buildings, big and little; it didn't matter. My job was assembly.

At first, I worked with a short, slight man whose attitude was much less than desirable. He was hard to please, a real company man, and I'm sure he would betray his own mother if it furthered his own position. My initial job was lining up fuse boxes. This consisted of working in the contacts inside the box so that they made full contacts. The box was metal, about a foot square, and the metal inside was copper designed to carry 440 volts.

The contacts looked like this **(Frank drew a photo that looked like a garlic clove with the "stem" on top).** The bar fits in the slot designated by the arrow. My job was to shape the tops with pliers so that perfect contact was made on the bar. To check this, we used a very thin piece of metal (a feeler) and tried to fit it into the space between the bar and the contact; if it fit in there, it had to be made shaping with the pliers. Then when we accomplished this, we rubbed a mixture of Vaseline and carbon on this point of contact and worked it up and down until it made grooves and caused a perfect fit. This was all wiped up and ready for shipment. (I'm sure that was about as interesting as sitting around watching paint dry). The description above was my first phase of the job.

My boss was just terrible, and there came a time that I had had enough, and it was either punch him out or quit the job. This filled my mind for a long time, and finally, it came to the point that I couldn't tolerate it anymore. I went to the office and told the superintendent that I couldn't work with

Sip; this was the guy's name. The superintendent's name was Joe, and he was half-owner of the plant.

His response surprised me, he said that he would put me in another department, and I should go back to work. When he showed me this attitude, I suddenly realized that there was a chance to make more money. The starting rate was 40 cents an hour. I thanked him for his confidence in me but told him I had another job in a bakery shop for more money. This was a concoction on my part.

He then offered me a raise of 2 and ½ cents an hour, which was the going rate at that time. He seemed so willing, it made me try a little harder, and I said the bakery job paid more than that. So, he gave me a nickel raise and sent me back to work. This raise was unheard of at that time. My next job was with a guy they called "the dago", and he was great to work for. We assembled airplane panels, and these were used for all of the main electrical controls in the airplane. About this time, Adolf Hitler was making noises in Europe, and this country was starting to produce planes and war equipment.

After working on this job for a time, I was moved to a really nice job and was my own boss. The foreman gave me a stack of blueprints for assembling slate panels. This work consisted of mounting copper bus bars on the pre-drilled slate panels, and you followed the blueprint for this. The slate was about an inch and a half thick and about 5" x 5" with holes drilled and countersunk. The copper bars were all made up, and it was my job to put it all together. Once assembled, I had to insulate the panel and then check it for shorts. This job kept me busy and was interesting. All told, I worked here 3 ½ years and made 67 and ½ cents an hour when I went into the Army (1942).

GIRL FROM ACROSS TOWN

One day I attended some type of event at the Cleveland Stadium. As I was walking out after the event, amidst the throngs of people, this beautiful blond girl stood out like an oasis in a desert. Seeing this girl was a brand-new experience for me. It isn't that I didn't experience pretty girls in the past, but this girl seemed to be the answer in every category. Yet, that last statement has to be a shallow and biased one. I didn't even know her – as yet – and all my conclusions were based exclusively on sight alone. Now, I stood enchanted; she could be gone in seconds, never to be seen again I could be left with my regrets.

My plan was simple enough; I would introduce myself to her and tell her of my interest, factually explaining that I wasn't an oddball on the make but simply mesmerized by her beauty. The plan worked, and she gave me her phone number to call her later in the evening. Her phone number formed an indelible mark on my memory, and it is still there to this day: Clearwater 4995. Later in the evening, I made the call with a lot of anticipation, causing the blood to coarse through my body. In a young man's life, this is the epitome of excitement and makes living a vital experience surpassing all others.

The first call was very fruitful and led to the first visit, which in turn resulted in an exciting relationship. She lived on Rocky River Drive, way across town on Sedalia Avenue. I had no transportation, so I rode the old-fashioned streetcar, which took a long time to get across town. Yet, this was not disturbing, and as a matter of fact, a normal facet of life and therefore acceptable. We dated, and her parents liked me very much. Her father was a big shot for the Dobeckman Company; he and I would shoot pool in his recreation room. At times, Dorothy would come downstairs and, in a perturbed voice, say, "Who did you come to visit, my father or me?" Our relationship developed into what I considered serious, not really knowing what she felt, and it crossed my mind to marry her someday. The times were getting turbulent, however, and the uncertainly was cause to wait.

DRAFTED

While I worked at the Powerlite Switchboard Company, I had to register for the draft, I received two, six-month deferments or I could have gone to the service a year earlier. Hitler was going crazy in Europe (1940-1942) and was picking off countries left and right. The mentality of the people of this country was almost a frenzied patriotism, and never was united as much as at that time. In the interim, Japan was also acting very hostile, and we were negotiating on serious terms with them. Yet, this particular Sunday evening, I was downtown on my way to the Palace Theater on Euclid Avenue to see a famous band, Jan Savrit. The news came out that Japan had attacked Pearl Harbor, December 7, 1941, and destroyed a large portion of our fle et.

Shortly after, we declared war on Germany and Japan. The military and industrial industry mobilized, both with a lot of vigor and righteous indignation. After my year of deferments at Powerlite Switchboard, President Franklin D. Roosevelt sent me my invitation to serve in the Armed Forces. This was an invitation that you just didn't refuse. I can honestly say that I was itching to go. Being twenty-two and full of vigor, dumb too, I looked for the adventure of war.

I was ordered to report to the Draft Board; there were many other young men of my age. We were all given an examination, and those who were classified 1-A were sworn in. The examination consisted of an assembly line-type procedure with each doctor having his particular station and one specific thing he examined. This expedited the examination, and they were rather thorough. The last doctor was a *psychiatrist* who seemed to be looking mainly for normal men with usual male inclinations. A point of interest here is that as I was going through the line, one of the first doctors asked me about my chest scars. We were stripped to the waist, and the scars were there for everyone to see. By this time, my phobia about them were passed.

He made me lift my arms and saw that there was some pulling and asked if that interfered in any way with my motion. I was advised to tell one of the doctors down the line if I had a problem with this. This interaction put me into a relatively mild dilemma of mixed emotion and confusion. Here was an opportunity to get turned down, yet I didn't know if I wanted that; part of me said yes. I had time to think as I made my way through the line and rationalized that 4F wasn't a stigma I wanted on myself. Four F was the term of rejections.

Secondly, I was curious as to what it would be like to be a soldier. My pride for my country also played a large part. When I reached the doctor, who would look over the scars, my presentation was feeble in my behalf of rejection since I wanted to go. Previously, my brother John had gone down to the Marine Corp. to sign up, but they turned him down for a cloudy eardrum. This rejection infuriated him, and he said, "the hell with them if they want me now, they'll have to draft me." They DID later, and he ended up in Fort Bragg, North Carolina, for the rest of the war, *never* going overseas.

So, I passed the physical and awaited the call. There was a white-hot fever all over the country, and I have never witnessed such enthusiasm and such unity as a nation. When the call came for me to go, the good-byes and the wet eyes needed no verbal explanation. There was normal apprehension and the doubt that nudges forward in the mind as to if we would ever see each other again. My assurances to them that I would be alright was hollow of course, for how could I know?

Yet my youth couldn't let me think negatively, and I was full of enthusiasm and optimism. The male animal thrives on challenge and adventure and seeks out the competition in one form or another. This was the competency of the first order. Of course, I was concerned about the financial status of my family. I was contributing all my pay at home to help with the mortgage. Even when I was in high school, I worked three days a week in a bakery to help out my mother and father. I wondered how I could help them with the small pay I would receive as a soldier. The pay started as thirty dollars a month and was designed to cover your bare necessities. Nonetheless, with all these thoughts, I was on my way.

CAMP PERRY

We boarded the train and went to Camp Perry, Ohio. There were long lines of railroad cars just loaded with the cream of the crop of the country's youth. Camp Perry is not too far from Cleveland, and the ride was just a matter of hours. You could feel all of the variety of emotions on the train ride, but by and large, you don't keep a bunch of young guys down. Soon there was horseplay coupled with the sound of the din that goes with it. No one wondered out loud as to what the future held, but the anticipation was tucked way in the dark corners of the mind.

Arriving at Camp Perry, we saw the rows upon rows of impersonal barracks, not designed to be impressive, and the builder succeeded totally. The barracks were clean and plain, no-frills, but sturdy. They housed double-decked cots and footlockers, which was the extent of our furniture. This place was just for testing and classification, and we all knew that Camp Perry was a jumping-off place. The very first night, when long lines closed in, and the realization that we were away from our beds and our loved ones permeated the mind, we sought other avenues of diversion.

One of the men, Kenny Farar, had been a professional entertainer in nightclubs. His talent included singing, playing the piano, and telling jokes, and we all ended up in a songfest in the social hall. We repeated these nights for as long as our stay at Camp Perry. Here too, is where the term KP became very meaningful. It was no longer an expression, but an action, a very personal action, with me the primary character actor. AFTER a 14-hour stint in the kitchen, you lost all your character, and the only thing left was action toward the cot. I mopped that huge floor at least three times that day, and each ensuing time a little slower.

Simply because when you finished the floor, they said do it again and again. There were pots and pans and dishes and silverware to scrub, and this was three times a day after each meal. Nothing lasts forever, and this day passed too. It was very impressive and is burned into my memory to this day. My turn came to be tested so they could classify me, along with hundreds of other guys. They interviewed us to discover our talents, experience, job training, and aptitudes.

There was an extended test involved in this with a variety of quizzes, word study, stories to test the mental prowess, and other multi-faceted gimmicks to check your scope of reasoning power. By and large, I passed the test well enough, and I realized this later when I was in Oregon. The First Sergeant said I was qualified for officer's training if I was so inclined.

In the interview itself, they asked what branch of service we would prefer. Then we were told to make two other choices in the event we didn't get the first choice. My first choice was the Signal Corps, my second choice was the Air Corps, and with prodding by my interviewer, my last choice was the Quartermaster Corps. Through my interview, he learned that I had had some bakery experience. He suggested this should be my third choice, so it was.

Now, I must confess that the Signal Corps held a fascination for me, and I knew it included stringing telephone lines in combat areas. This seemed like fun and adventurous participating in the war effort, so I picked THAT. If this didn't materialize, I thought the Air Corps had some glamour to it, and that would be all right too. The other, being a baker, didn't sound exciting at all, yet not being entirely stupid, I could see many advantages there. This is where the matter rested, and we would not find out our status until we went to our next destination for training.

The day came soon enough for us to ship out, and the friendships hastily made were severed abruptly. All of the loneliness came storming back in, and it really was a sentimental journey. My contingent was being sent to Virginia as I discovered, and as we headed South, and further and further from home. All I could think of was the girl I left behind and, of course, my family and all that was familiar to me.

SHIPPING OUT

The picture should be a little clearer now as to my disconcerted mental state, with all emotions of loneliness coming into play. I mentioned the phrase "sentimental journey" in previous chapters. It carried double importance since there was a song by that name currently popular playing on the train. With its rhythmic clickity-clack, the train sped southward further and further from home to the draftees' destination. When we arrived in Virginia, it was raining, and the temperature was considerably warmer. This stays in my memory since Cleveland weather wasn't that great at that time of the year.

After getting off the train, and there were many of us, we just stood around for a while, as we became a part of this organized confusion. After some time, they got to us, and this was to be the pattern of the Army – Hurry up and wait. The man in charge told us our various instructions, and I ended up in a pyramidal tent all by myself. A pyramidal tent is a large tent housing six men, made of dark green waterproof canvas, with six cots embraced a dirt floor. The lost feeling overwhelmed me, and I fell across one of the cots and cried. Tears don't last forever, and the relief they bring is good. I felt better, not great, but better, and soon five other men came into the tent and were to be my new family. It didn't take long to get acquainted, and the expression "misery loves company" fits very well here.

The next day, they called out all of the new arrivals were en masse; an officer addressed us and explained why we were there. The seriousness of war, and even mentioned that some of us would be KILLED before the war ended. He said they would train us well, and this training would help keep us alive.

This camp in Virginia was called Camp Lee and was the primary training center for the Quartermaster Corps. It soon became apparent to me that I would be trained as a baker for the army. The prerequisite to this was to become a soldier. There was an emphasis on being a well-trained soldier since it unknown when they might call on us to fight. We were given six weeks of basic training. The Infantry and other fighting units received three to six months of training since this was their main activity.

The six-week basic training program is like entering into a different world, a world considerably worse, but one so full of activity. There was little time to think of anything else. This training period was intense and seemed to the civilian mind as irrational, irresponsible, and stupid. From the beginning, it appeared purely illogical, lacked totally in sensitivity. There was an emphasis on time or the lack of it; we were pressed on and on into the soldier state of mind. This frame of mind eradicates the civilian complacency with slow, subtle anger that makes you want to fight.

The service, when training, leaves nothing to chance. Whenever we learned a new exercise or a soldier-related maneuver, it was always by the numbers. This mindset relates to everything from exercise and gas mask drills to marching or bayonet practice. The only thing exempt was sleeping and eating, and sometimes I thought eating should have been included in that, simply to temper the voracious appetites coupled with the total lack of manners. Now the pace was very fast. We had to learn marching, how to shoot a gun, the manual of arms, and how to do anything that took at least ten minutes when in a hurry, to do it in two minutes.

The marching had to be in unity, and this taught us to act as a unit. There was the right-face, left face, to the rear march, eyes right, eyes left, half, at ease, on the oblique and attention. There was a thing called "the about-face," that many guys had trouble with because some people have two left feet. Another course we went through for physical fitness was called the "obstacle course." The name itself generally explains the gist of the course. To be more specific, we did the course on the run. There would be a narrow board across a brook, the board being possibly three inches wide, and the course dictated we run across on this board.

A lot of the training soldiers ran the rest of the course, dripping wet. There were corrugated metal tunnels to crawl thru, and overhead bars to swing across, right over another brook that rapidly coursed ahead with its very cold waters ready to engulf a falling soldier. They made this course over the same brook apparently because shortly after that, we were challenged by a heavy rope suspended from a tree. To get across, we had to take a running swing with the rope and make like a bird, landing rather suddenly, if not abruptly, on the other side. The daddy of them all was this high wooden structure built at least two stories tall, about 15 feet square.

It was draped over by a huge rope ladder that extended on all sides from top to bottom. The purpose was to climb to the top on one side and then crawl down from the other side. This course gave the butterflies a chance to stir in the stomach, but we weren't permitted to think about it since they rushed us through. Later I realized the importance of this exercise, *since I did the very same thing going into the invasion of France,* crawling down the side of the boat, or ropes formed in squares for a ladder effect.

Of course, no obstacle course could be complete without the high wall to climb, assisted by the long rope hanging down. The trick was to climb up with the rope, with your feet on the wall walking upward. Once you reached the top, you were on your own; the jump down was tempered by sawdust on the bottom of the other end. There were other innovations too, but they do not come readily to mind, but these descriptions should be sufficient to give the proper concept of the course.

In practice with the gas masks, we had to go through it, step by step, over and over, by the numbers. The admonitions were that we would eventually be placed in a room full of tear gas with our masks off. Then it would be necessary to know how to put the masks on under pressure. They kept their word, and one day they instructed us as to how we were to act. We were to enter the room. Before entering, they told us to fill our lungs with air and step into the room holding our breath. At the command, we were to take one sniff, and at the following command, put our masks on. Just ONE sniff was sufficient to make us value our gas masks because tear gas is terrible, causing choking and profuse tearing of the eyes.

Camp Lee was a huge place and could have been compared to a small city. There were rows and rows of barracks and street upon street upon street. They were all characteristically the same and were marked according to company and unit. There were other buildings for administration, and occasionally a small home stood out haughtily and had a prominence by itself against the monotonous background of barracks. The small home with grass and flowers was for the regular army men who were married sergeants and lived there on the base.

RANK EXPLAINED

My platoon had as the head, a buck sergeant and a corporal below him. The officer was a lieutenant who acts as a chief honcho and really placed fear in your heart with his untouchable militaristic aloofness. To save anyone reading this the trouble, I will incorporate some facts as to rank and names of units of service since then, these accounts of my army activities will be more understandable.

A platoon is made of four squads, and each squad has eight men. This makes 32 men in a quartermaster platoon. The *infantry* has a *different* arrangement, and their platoon is twice the size of a Quartermaster unit. Each squad has a squad leader, and he may either be a corporal or a private first class. The head of the four squads is a buck sergeant.

The description given here is of our training unit at Camp Lee. Later, when we formed our bakery company, there were some differences in rank, but not in the size of the platoon.

To have a clearer understanding of rank, here is a detailed account from private to general. A private has no stripes, a PFC or a private first class has one stripe, and his pay is slightly higher.

Each rank assures better pay and more responsibility. A corporal has two stripes and is the direct liaison to the buck sergeant, who has three stripes. The next rank is staff sergeant, which is three stripes on top and one on the bottom.

The next rank is a technical sergeant with three stripes on top and two at the bottom. Top sergeant, or master sergeant, or first sergeant are one and the same. This sergeant has three stripes on top and three on the bottom. When he is the head of a company, he usually is referred to as a first sergeant. Master sergeants serve in different capacities, and not all are first sergeants of companies.

The next rank is sort of a no-man's land, and he is called a warrant officer. He resides between a non-commissioned officer and a commissioned officer. Up to this point, all ranks mentioned were non-commissioned. Now my knowledge of a warrant officer is limited, but I know that rank is by the appointment of the Secretary of War and is not commissioned.

The next category of all officers listed are all commissioned by the President of the United States. These men must be of superior intelligence and possess qualities of leadership and abilities to make decisions satisfactorily.

In essence, these are the required qualifications desired, yet to become an officer is one of the options. Many qualified men of superior intelligence and other qualities never applied for officers' training simply because they were not so inclined. Those who DID apply went to special officer training schools, and upon graduation, they were given their commission as a second lieutenant, signified by one gold bar. The training course took three months. This term "ninety-day wonder" was born in reference to a brand-new second lieutenant who was usually overrated to his new rating and tried to act authoritatively without any finesse!

A second lieutenant was generally held in poor regard by the enlisted men, but this was done with discretion and secret since we were subject to the officer's authority, and disobedience was a serious offense that could be punishable by court-martial. In turn, it would result in incarceration in the stockade. In fairness to the American soldier, they were, in large part, good men and obedient.

Moving along in rank, the next in line was a first lieutenant who wore one silver bar. They were usually more settled through experience and consequently more respected. A captain has two silver bars on each shoulder and usually commands a company.

The lieutenants had a platoon each and are responsible to the captain. There are four platoons to a company, four companies to a battalion. A battalion is headed by a major who wears a gold oak leaf. Next in line is a lieutenant colonel who wears a silver oak leaf and is called colonel, NOT lieutenant colonel. The colonel and the lieutenant colonel are of very high rank and command a corps, which I believe consists of four battalions, but I'm not certain. A FULL colonel wears a silver eagle and is just below a general.

In the category of general, a brigadier general wears one star and could be in charge of an army. Incidentally, I skipped a "division" category that fits into the notch after battalion since two or more divisions make a corps. Anyway, the largest single-unit ends up being an army, and generals command that.

After a brigadier general follows the major general with two stars, then a lieutenant general with three stars, and a full general with four stars, another rank was created with five stars, and there were only two of those rare birds: General MacArthur and General Eisenhower. They were in charge of a theater of operation, which in this case was the European Theater (World War II) and the Far Eastern Theater.

My immediate concern was not with all these men of high rank but with my platoon's buck sergeant and corporals. They were very impressive men who commanded respect and obedience simply by their appearance, which personified the military at its best. To say that I was in awe of these superior officers would not understate this fact. Together with the pre-conceived notion I had before entering the service; this impression worked for my benefit in the long-range of things.

Before going into service, it was established in my mind that I would be in the minority as a soldier. They had their ways, and no one was going to change that. Secondly, I realized that, if possible, I should gain from this experience. This included gaining a broader outlook on life as it progressed in other areas and gaining materially as well. So, I had decided to do as I was told and make the best of whatever came my way. This gift of acceptance made me more comfortable with myself and times more bearable.

Let this not be an inference that I took on a robot's status since many things happened in the service that appeared senseless if not plain "idiotic." Yet, the most senseless thing on my part would be to challenge them while they are holding four aces and me with a pair of deuces and nothing wild. This strategy worked well, as you shall see in the ensuing chapters.

ARMY HIKE, CANTEENS

My objective now was to learn the system and master everything that was taught. This attitude was of great benefit in basic training. For example, we would be told we are going out for a long hike that would cover twenty miles. They reminded us to make sure our canteens were full of water because the day was hot, the roads dusty, and the sweat would pour. They were right on all these counts. I could add a few more things to that as the feet, and the legs became wearier, and the blisters began to form. We carried a fully loaded pack on our shoulders, and as we plodded on, there was an awareness of the straps pulling the shoulders and doing their best to cut into the flesh.

After arriving at a pre-designated point, possibly ten miles out, we were told to stop and take a break. There were firm instructions given not to touch the drinking water except on command. All of us sat down in this wooded area seeking the coolest spot available and at the same time lighted up a cigarette. "Smoke if you got them" was an order presented to us as well. The army way is not the civilian way, just the opposite. No sooner were we given the order to rest and smoke, we were told to get up and put out our cigarettes.

We fell back into ranks and were ordered to follow these simple instructions "by the numbers." On the count of one, place your hand on your canteen, count of two, take out the canteen and hold it in front of you. On the count of three, unscrew the top of the canteen, and on the count of four, turn the canteen upside down and dump ALL the drinking water on the ground. This command, measured in strictly logical terms, was stupidly brutal and shockingly insensitive. We followed orders like good soldiers and watched as that precious water streamed recklessly to the ground. The parched throats that seemed just bearable before this broke out in a flagrant rebellion that dried up the last ounce of saliva. Truly now, we were spitting dust. Of course, there was a method to this madness as we learned mental toughness and self-discipline for survival.

However, the lesson was lost at that particular moment and was replaced by a great deal of seething, smoldering, but silent anger! Needless to say, the walk back seemed like a thousand miles, like it would never end, but nothing lasts forever, and we finally arrived at the camp in insatiable thirst. Before being told to fall out, they instructed us to go to our barracks and remain there for blister inspection. At the order to fall out, everyone made a dash for the water, sore feet and all, ran, yes, RAN at top speed! This moment was pure delight, and water never tasted so good!!!

The activities of basic training are so demanding that it leaves little room for thought. It opened the door for many other emotions to come into play, mainly the negative ones, and added to a bad situation. All this excessive activity did accomplish one basic truth: Homesickness started to melt away, and the mid-set started to zero in on reality. This was war, it is serious business, a matter of grave importance, and we had better start thinking that way. The continued emphasis was on mental toughness, stoked by lingering anger that negated complacency. All of our activities were interspersed with this objective in mind.

Take, for instance, this case: We were out in the field marching, after a while, we came back to camp. In the camp yard, we were told we had ten minutes to relax in our tents. When we returned, we were to have our outer jackets inside and our inner shirt on the outside. In other words, just the reverse as it had been before. To the logical mind, this is nonsense, but no one ever asked us how we felt about it. To spice up the matter, just a minute or two had gone by when the fall out commander sounded. This was far short of the time mentioned that we were allowed, and men came scrambling out changing shirts as they ran to add to this mirthless confusion. Realize this: The incentive of motivation would always be the avoidance of some kind of punishment.

When told to do something, the army always meant RIGHT NOW! The punishments for lackadaisical response took on many forms, were promptly administered, and without any outward display of conscience or remorse. There could be kitchen patrol (KP), which five in the morning until eight at night, latrine duty, which involved cleaning toilets and floors and subject to inspection. If they don't pass, you do it all over again.

Policing the area or in lay terms going all over the area picking up all refuse laying around, cigarette butts, etc. There were other weird punishments too that made no sense, were unproductive, and served no purpose. Had this been done in civilian life, the perpetrator would have been a candidate for the psych ward.

All of these things I mention are to establish a true concept in your mind as to the army mentality and their methods of preparing a person for war. Thus, it should be understood that this is a factual report of how it was here, how I felt about it and how it had to be. The system worked because, at the end of the training period, we all were in a fighting mood and stayed that way. It should be pointed out that in all other aspects, we were taken care of in the vital essentials. We changed our beds with regularity, showered regularly, ate very well, and were well clothed. We had our proper rest and had a specific time for bed and a specific time to rise.

CLEANLINESS

The cleanliness aspect was of vital importance since we all lived together in the barracks. We slept in double-decked cots, and the man on top slept just the opposite of the man on the bottom cot. This was an army directive, and I could see the credence in that system. Beds had to be made upon arising and pulled tight so that a quarter would bounce up if dropped. Regular showers were required so that each man maintained reasonable cleanliness. This rule generally was adhered to without any required pre-empting, but there always will be a non-conformist in the crowd. We told the sergeant amount this guy who would not bathe, and he said we should bathe him, but first, give fair warning. We had just run out of fair warning, however, and it now was time to act.

We cornered this guy, armed with a GI brush and a GI bar of soap, dragged him to the shower room. A GI brush is a stiff-bristled brush used for general scrubbing, and GI soap was a powerful brown soap for any type of cleaning. We soaked him with water and soaped up the brush, scrubbing the hell out of him with him still in his clothes. This guy got the message, and we didn't have that problem again. We just told him when to take a bath, and he went right to it.

We usually had scrambled eggs, fried potatoes, coffee, oatmeal and bread, and milk to drink for breakfast. Sometimes we had a variation of bacon, sausage, and a thing we called "shit on a shingle." This was toasted bread with a white sauce poured over the bread, and the sauce had hamburger meat in it. The breakfasts were huge, and you could go for seconds if you wish. Keep in mind that this was going on at 6:30 in the morning since we were called out for roll call at 5:45 am. Everybody had better be there and on time, or it would be just too bad. Then, we all had to line up, and our sergeant checked us all out. When he was called upon to report, he snapped to attention and said, "All present and accounted for, Sir!" This report was accompanied by a brisk salute since the report was being delivered to an officer of our platoon.

The report was relayed up and down the line until the entire company was accounted for. The final report was given to the captain by the first sergeant who said, "Company present and accounted for!" with a brisk military salute. We were then dismissed and went to wash up and shave, etc., and get ready for breakfast.

All calls were made by the sound of the bugle, and each activity had its own particular scale of notes. There was a call for getting up, and a call for going to bed, mail call, chow call (eat), assembly call. There was a call at six p.m. that you responded to by turning to the flag and saluting no matter what you were doing at the time, just as long as it was an outside activity. The clothing was of the finest quality, and the footwear was sturdy and comfortable.

The order of the day was strict regimentation, yet without it would be disorder and chaos. One sunny day during our basic training, we were called to fall out and always on the double. No one loafed anyway, but the army always wanted it a LITTLE faster than that. We were set in the formation and marched out into a field of grass, and the topography was fairly flat. Orders were given to file cut in columns of two, which created a rather long line.

BOXING

There was a suggestion as to what was about to happen because off on the side was a huge pile of boxing gloves. It became more and more apparent that we were to become the participants at a certain sport. Both columns of men were given the halt command, and one line was given the right face and the other a left face. Each line now stood face to face with one another. At about this time, my heart fluttered and sank because standing opposite me was the biggest, huskiest guy, I EVER saw. In a fleeting instance and in its wildest imagination, my mind perceived myself being matched with this brute in a boxing match, which the army conceived at random. That was just for one instant, but then logic kicked in, and I realized that such an arrangement was ridiculous, a positive mismatch, and I relaxed, but just for a moment.

The sergeant in charge bellowed out in an authoritative voice, "You box the man you are facing!" My wildest imagination and deepest fears swept in and overwhelmed me. Turning to the sergeant, and at the same time beckoning to this hulk in front of me, I shouted, "You gotta be kidding!" His answer, and without hesitation, was, "FIGHT HIM!" Had I had any inkling, whatever kind of day it would be, I would either have stayed in bed forgone on sick call. It was too late for anything like that now, and I was about to be led to the slaughter.

While they were bringing over the gloves, I had to think of a plan to avoid total disaster. He had the longest arms I've ever seen, and they looked the size of hams. The fear ever amplified this even further, and everything looked gigantic, yet I realized if I got inside his arms, he couldn't hit me with one of those trip hammers. The rest of the men were also aware of this catastrophic event and even stopped to watch.

There was nothing I could really do, so I decided to use the element of surprise and go on the offensive. All this time, the big guy never said a word. At the command to fight, my plan was to rush right in and dig a right to the center of his stomach with all the force I could muster, then cross over with a round-house left to the chin. This plan would surprise him or maybe get him mad; then I'd be in a hell of a shape. There was no other way, let alone turn yellow since I'd never live it down. Suddenly the command to fight came, and I wasted no time.

With all the force I could muster, my right glove dug deeply into his mid-section. There was a grunt and a burst of escaping air, his knees buckled a little, and his chin came forward. By this time, I was launching a left-handed rocket from the ground up and deposited the accumulated force directly on his protruding chin. At this point, you always step back a little to survey the situation and plan the rest of your attack accordingly.

This guy went down and out like a giant oak crashing to the ground to my joy, satisfaction, and relief. My secret hope was he wouldn't get up because I'm sure I could only take one punch from that guy, and I'm through. His lights went out, however, and so did all of the fight in him; just to be on the safe side, I helped him up. After all, I didn't know the guy, and I didn't want any enemies.

The fight was planned by the army, and we were victims of the circumstance. All of the other men had seen this happen, and they were filled with awe. The rest of my stay at camp life was just great! Word spread like WILDFIRE, and I was treated like some kind of celebrity. Lucky for me, there were no more fights scheduled, for my bubble would have burst somewhere along the line. I could fight fairly well, better than average, but this had been like a fantasy, and I liked the illusion.

REPORT TO THE SERGEANT

About three weeks into our basic training, the sergeant singled me out and told me to report to him at the end of the day. This command was a shock to me since a man of such importance would not have any dealings with a mere enlisted man unless he messed up somehow. The rest of the day was not very pleasant as I mulled over in my mind where I had gone wrong.

The fateful time came, and I trudged toward the sergeant's quarters with a heavy heart anticipating the worst. The imagination can really bend things out of shape; I was sure I would be shot at the very least. I knocked on this door since he had a private room, and he told me to enter in a pleasant way, which allayed my feelings somewhat. I thought maybe this was like the last meal before execution. He asked me to sit down and still acted sociable; my fears had now turned to curiosity, a burning, nagging curiosity that needed to be fulfilled. It turned out to be simple enough.

He said he had been watching me, that I learned my soldiering well, and there was no more need for me to train. As of that moment, he said I was now promoted to squad leader. A few days later, I was called in again. This time he told me that he was taking me out of the hot sun, and I could finish the rest of my basic training in the orderly room (the company office) as a mail clerk. My job now was to sort mail in their proper pigeonholes and deliver them to their destination all over camp. Part of the job was to get the payroll book signed each month. Each month, it was a policy of the government to have your signature in the payroll book before you would be paid. This job took me all over Camp Lee, looking for these people to sign the book. The sergeant said it was too much walking, so he got a bike for me to ride. This job was a real snap, and as it turned out, all the time I spent in the service only resulted in KP for me just one time. That was great because KP was lousy!

As I write along, it is amazing the things I can recall, but then, there is no doubt countless numbers of other things forgotten and unrecorded. The fact is that these incidents stand out in my mind and are the most impressionable. In this narration, there may be a repetition here and there, and I ask for your tolerance simply because these accounts are spread over many, many days. There could be justifiable cause for some repetition, but really not much, if at all.

BIBLE GIVEN

Now, I don't recall if I mentioned receiving a small Bible from the army, but I must mention it here because this book put me in touch with the reality of who God is. This was not apparent when I picked up the book; neither was there a flash of lightning or the rumble of thunder. When I opened the book, I was exposed to the truth. When I read, which was seldom, I liked what I read. God takes His time with people and draws them along at various paces, according to the person, who He knows better than the person knows himself. This book was put together for the Catholic church and was composed differently.

The scriptures are the scriptures according to the gospel, but they are put together with a continuity that follow a line of thought. In other words, they take a line from Paul and could follow with a line from Peter or John, but it constitutes the complete thought. Each line is marked down from where it came from, and to me, this is very helpful. The book is in my possession to this day. It is over forty-five years old, and I have it taped up as needed.

My age at this time is sixty-six, and my birthday comes on January 17th of each year. I was born in the year 1920. The government also made up Bibles for the other faiths that were represented in the service. I know for a fact that there was a Jewish Bible and a Protestant version. There may have been others for other faiths, but I am not aware of this for a fact, but logic dictates there would be.

In the service, we met many people from different walks of life. At Camp Lee, I met a man from Virginia who I got to know as a friend. We were quite compatible in our likes and dislikes, solace in each other's miseries, and found comfort in our sharing, both talking and listening. This man, I later found, was an influential person, one of means, educated, and was traveling in the elite circle. This didn't occur to me through any of his own doing since he kept a low profile, didn't brag or put on airs, and acted mainly as just one of the guys.

At this point, let me clarify one point. It was nice to meet people of influence, but I liked just about anyone I met and never looked for status or importance in a person. There too, were some that I didn't identify with and never got to know. This rule of thumb works both ways, and I' sure there was some who wouldn't identify with me either. This is good because there are all kinds of people with all sorts of likes and dislikes and various personalities - nevertheless, on with my story.

WANT TO MEET GIRLS?

This man, whose name I forgot, had apparently been screening me, and I must have passed the test. One evening, after all, our chores were done, we settled back to relax in our particular corner of the barracks. Then he said he knew some girls in town and asked if I would be interested in spending a Sunday afternoon visiting with them. This question was like asking a man in the desert, parched with thirst, if he would like a glass of sparkling, cool, crystal-clear water and all you could drink. The answer, of course, was an emphatic YES, then it was a matter of waiting for that day in pleasant anticipation.

Sunday came, and he was true to his word. We went to this girl's home, and there were three other girls there as well. We spent a very enjoyable afternoon playing records, dancing, and some light refreshment. There was a girl that appealed to me, I asked her if I could see her again, and she said fine. She gave me her address and phone number. When my next day off rolled around, which always was Sunday, I called the number the girl provided me and was very relieved to hear that she would like to go out Sunday.

The day came along slowly as it seemed, and I looked for an escape from the camp and to escape my loneliness. Being with all men for weeks on end leaves something to be desired, and I knew just what that desire was. Leaving camp that Sunday, I felt an exhilaration that leaves a boy a little giddy. My step was springier, and my gait quicker. There was, however, a big surprise for me that I could not have possibly imagined even in my wildest dreams!

SO I TOOK A CAB

Getting off the base, I called a cab and told him to drive me to the number she had given me. We started out driving a long way, and suddenly we were out in the country. This led me to wonder if the cab driver knew his way or had gotten lost. I questioned him, and he assured me that he was heading to the location of that number. Sometime later, as we drove along, I looked up the road and saw a large plantation complete with the huge white house and elegantly majestic columns gracing the home's front. It crossed my mind to wonder what people who lived in houses like that were like.

I remembered my history lessons in school and seeing this was like entering another zone or dimension, with its mystics causing awe of wonderment. As these thoughts ran over the keyboard of my mind, I was brought back to reality very abruptly. instead of driving past this magnificent mansion, the cab driver was pulling into the long drive that led directly to the white supporting pillars. "Hey, where are you going?" I said with alarm, "This has to be the wrong place!" "This IS the address you gave me, Sir," the driver answered. "Well, pull up to the door, and I'll ask if the young lady lives there," was my reply, with an unsteadiness that suggested a mild panic.

Suddenly the quickened step evaporated, and the spring had sprung. My progress to the door was dampened by the fact that I knew she just *couldn't* live here! She was very nice and well-mannered and a lady in all respects, but she also impressed me as being too warm and too human to live on a plantation. Besides, I'm just a little old city boy born of ethnic parents who lived very poorly, below the poverty level all of the time. While all these feelings were crushing my brain like falling dominoes, I was at the door using the metal knocker heralding my presence, and at the same time, wishing it weren't so loud, and I could leave because no one answered.

This huge beautiful door slowly opened, and just like a script in a movie, a butler was standing there in his starched stance and utterly proper, regaled in formal wear, looking at me as if I were an intruder. "Yes?" he inquired. "Pardon me, but I should like to know if a Miss ___ lives here?" I questioned timidly. The butler said she did and asked, "Who shall I say is calling please?" He asked me to step into the small waiting room by the door, and when he learned my name, stepped up to the main doors to the next spacious room, and announced in a loud voice, "Mr. Traska (or Private Traska in this case) is calling for Miss ___."

Introductions to the parents followed, and shortly after, the young lady came skipping along, full of vim and vitality and still very human at ease. She greeted me very warmly, and all my anxieties melted away. After the customary chit-chat between her parents and myself, we got into the cab and drove off. A really different kind of day, I thought to myself.

This was a very impressive happening and the date itself was very nice. We went to town to see a movie and the army service club, where there were many accommodations for soldiers at that time. There was music, dancing, food, and places to relax and talk. As I look back in retrospect, I wonder why our relationship didn't further itself. Yet as I search the hidden corners of my mind and reflect on my state of mind at that time, I can see too many mental blocks that would have negated a pursuit of this course. She was very obviously wealthy; I was still writing to Dorothy Gedeon with fervor and dedication. My future was uncertain, and I wasn't seeking any binding relations with anyone at that time. I could have corresponded with her briefly, but this ended soon, and the matter was filed in my memory as a pleasant if not unnerving experience.

TRAINING SCHOOL

Time has a way of moving along, and our basic training came to an end. It was time now to enter into the second phase of our training. Each man was sent to a pre-determined school. There were many since Camp Lee was set up to train technicians of various sorts. My school, as I suspected, was the cooks and baker's school. At this phase of my life, my baking knowledge was minimal, yet at that time, I thought I knew a lot. This was that confident attitude I had that got me in a bind at times since I'd end up in situations where I had to back up my words with action. As I reflect now on that attitude, it had to be a mask or a front to cover up my inadequacies.

The school consisted of an area with about ten "tents." Actually, it was a plot of ground with about ten buildings on it. They were built of wood and the same size as a pyramidal tent. Each tent contained the tools of the trade for each occupation taught. In our area, baking was being taught, and each tent had a designated function that was covered. We learned how to roll bread, make a loaf, fire an oven, make a dough, etc.

BASICALLY, THIS BAKERY SCHOOL IS BENEATH MY INTELLIGENCE

The first day I was in school, this cockiness in me started to assert itself again. I looked at the teachers in the school and decided that I'm just as qualified as they are and should be a teacher and not a student. At the end of the day, just before I was to go back to camp, I saw the officer in charge of the school, a high-ranking Major. Approaching him, I presented my best military manner and requested permission to speak to him. This manner of conduct was extremely unusual for an enlisted man to pursue, and the consequences were not assured as related to a favorable conclusion.

This Major, fortunately, was polite and congenial, and attentive. I started, "Sir, I am a student at this school, but I feel that I have the qualifications to be a teacher here since this has been my trade." He was still listening, so I continued, "I feel that my talent is being wasted in the capacity of a student and could be instructing the other students in a meaningful capacity." After a few questions, the Major said he could get back to me and let me know. I thanked him and went on my way, not thinking anything would come of this since when the army sets its ways, it was just like being set in concrete. The next morning when I went into school, I had the shock of my life.

BE CAREFUL WHAT YOU WISH FOR; YOU MIGHT GET IT

The Major was there and took me to a tent and said, "This is your tent, teach." To be very honest, I wasn't qualified to teach and was lacking in many areas. A general knowledge of baking was all I had to fall back on, and this wasn't much. I knew the difference between a rolling pin and a yard stick, but the techniques were vague to me, and the panic I experienced was real and warranted. My class was set up to teach men to roll dough in balls and mold a loaf. I couldn't do this very well, so I embarked on a plan of bravado out of sheer desperation.

The first class that came in had about eight men: percentages told me that one of the eight had to be a baker. So, I said, "Does anyone here have any bakery experience?" One man said he had been a baker for ten years. "Well," I answered, "Show these men how to roll dough and make a loaf of bread," and continued, "I've been doing this so long it gets very boring." You know, it worked, and I learned with them! In a short time in my crash course, I became a real instructor and knew what I was talking about, but it was a big risk.

I really can't pre-suppose what would have happened had I been exposed as a fraud, but the embarrassment would have been the very least of it, I'm sure. A lesson was in the order here, and there was a sobering effect that I absorbed. There is an adage that says "nothing ventured, nothing gained," but I'm sure this applies to a person who at least knows what he is doing. My appropriate adage would be, "Fools rush in where angels fear to tread." At any rate, whatever has a cause affects, and this incident applies to the rule.

However, this is putting the cart before the horse, so let us see how this drama unfolds as this narration progresses. I feel that it is important to touch on some of the school's activities. It was an army school, and whereas baking is basic in its aspects, the innovations can take on other facets dictated by the environment and unusual conditions. Army baking certainly entered into "unusual circumstances" since the army baker was expected to produce under *any* conditions. We had our ingredients for baking: dry yeast, flour, sugar, salt, and milk powder.

COOKING IN THE FIELD

There also were portable ovens that were fired with a unit that fit in the bottom section of the oven. The unit used white gas that was very effective but had to be maintained properly. We had a course in repairing the maintaining these units as well. There was a project designed to awaken our imagination and versatility. They presented us with this problem: If your equipment was destroyed in the field, and all you had left were these ingredients, and a limited time, you were ordered to supply a unit with bread, what would your course of action be?

The answer certainly wasn't that we couldn't because we are inoperable. The army slogan burnt into our minds was "we can do anything, and the impossible takes a little longer." To get us started, they demonstrated how to mix the dough in the field. There was a hollow made into the ground as close to a half-sphere as possible. A section of a pup tent is then laid across this hole, and the ingredients are mixed in this concave enclosure. Each soldier carried half of a pup tent in his pack. When a tent needed to be pitched, two soldiers combined and snapped two sections together and had a whole tent.

Now that we had the method to make a dough, we were told that the field problem was to go out in the wilderness with the basic ingredients and bake bread. We were loaded onto trucks and taken out to "no man's land," given all the ingredients, and told that they would be back in the evening for the bread. My group consisted of about eight men, and each group was to use its ingenuity to arrive at the ultimate result: baked bread, fit to eat. I was in charge of this contingent, so I sent out a detail of men to search for a bank of soil about six or eight feet high, preferably one consisting of clay, and hurry back as soon as they found one.

It wasn't long that some men reported a spot such as this that had eroded through heavy rainstorms. We carried a trenching shovel with us as part of our equipment, and I instructed the men to dig into the bank. About three feet from the top, carefully hollowing out the interior to form a hole inside the bank with a floor, and the hole should be about two feet in height.

Carefully digging out his hole, we succeeded in accomplishing this. An opening in this bank's side extended in and around about six to seven feet, about two feet high. The hole was about six inches across from the top extending downward into the main chamber as the main exhaust for smoke and air circulation. Other men had been dispatched to gather wood and dry grass, and we had a dough started. Dry grass was placed into the hole with dry starter twigs and ignited.

As the flames grew in intensity, we added heavier wood and kept this up to "burn the hole out," seal up any loose dirt that could fall, and of course, retain enough heat for baking. When the fire had burned to the point that we thought was sufficient, we swept out all of the fire from the hole with some green branches we cut beforehand. Then a hand count was taken to determine the temperature of our make-shift oven. "Hand count" refers to the method where the hand is extended into the oven with fingers outstretched, then the person counts slowly: one one thousand, two one thousand, three one thousand, four one thousand as the proper temperature. As the hand was extended in the oven, if the fingers started to pinch and burn at the very tips, four one thousand indicated a temperature of about 450 degrees F., just right for baking.

In a make-shift oven such as this, we, of course, did not expect perfect results. We would be satisfied with ANY results. But it must be said that there are two kinds of heat in an oven: flash heat and other solid heat. Flash heat is the heat that floats around in the oven in a free-lancing manner, very similar to the heat found in a kitchen range, the heat that greets you when you open the door. Solid heat is built into the walls and is released slowly and steadily. The convection of solid heat is the desirable condition for steady even baking and uniform browning. Flash heat bakes the loaf exterior too quickly, tends to seal off the rest of the loaf, and could leave the center of the loaf unbaked.

I mention some of these factors since it is important to know about the problems encountered in the field away from controlled conditions. One of the biggest factors involved was the proper treatment of the yeast. Yeast has its own characteristics and abides by strict laws unwaveringly. To get the yeast to produce the proper results, you must play by its rules. To play by its rules, we should know what it is, what it expects, and how it reacts to stimuli or lack thereof. (It crosses my mind that if we dealt with people this way, it would be a giant step toward better understanding.)

First, what is it? It is a one-celled fungus found in the air around us, but there are many strains, and they are referred to as "wild." The cultured or refined strain is removed from the batch of foam or froth and accumulated for future use. In fresh yeast, it is usually trapped in starch as found in your everyday store-bought yeast. (I hope the reader isn't bored with this treatise on yeast, but in fairness, I must mention these things to give an impact tour field problem.) Yeast is affected by hot and by cold, salt and sugar, and responds accordingly.

Excessively prolonged periods of heat kills yeast, yet warmth from between 78 and 80 degrees is ideal for its growth and development. Sugar is the food that yeast cells thrive on but in controlled amounts. An extreme excess of sugar drives them into a type of hiding called reverting back to the "spore stage." They don't die; they just become inert and wait for more favorable conditions. With the proper amount of sugar, they eat and develop in a rapid and somewhat uncontrolled manner. This is why a controlled amount of salt is added to keep the cells mannerly and stable. Too much salt will drive them into the spore stage, and all activity will cease. In order to arrive at the proper results, all factors must be in balance. This is a natural law that remains constant, as are other natural laws that regulate our universe. All of creation has no problem with this; it all follows the natural law. Mankind is the exception to the rule and goes about its rebellious way attempting to break, bend or change the rules. As a result, man's history has been severely blemished from the beginning of time. Most pitifully, he pursues the same course and never learns from these past mistakes.

However, let us return to yeast, but I must warn you that I will deviate into a related essay that is stimulated by the narration in process.

Yeast reproduces itself in 120 minutes. An ounce will become two ounces in 120 minutes if the food is available and all conditions are favorable and correct. As long as the food source remains, the cell continues to produce, and once the food source is expanded, they start eating themselves. They are cannibalistic in nature, and when this happens, we call this a rotting process. Yeast in a bread dough causes fermentation, so as they eat, the sugar byproducts of CO2 (carbon dioxide) are released as alcohol. These gases season the dough by aerating it and also strengthens an ingredient in the dough itself called gluten. The gluten becomes more pliable and takes on a rubbery consistency that enables the bread to rise without collapsing.

In the oven, the primary rise is initiated by the escape and expansion of carbon dioxide and alcohol. Still, since yeast is killed at 120 degrees, another action takes over to assure the bread properly rises, called "diastatic action," which ceased to function at 140 degrees since the heat destroys that too. There is so much more I could write about baking, but it diverts from the flow of the story, and the extensive foray of baking facts really belong in a category of their own.

Now back to the open field and the good fresh country air. The dough has risen and has been shaped into round two-pound balls, and the oven is ready. The army requires this weight; only under certain circumstances did we make a one-pound loaf. Usually, this was when we made pan bread. We placed the bread into the improvised oven with an improvised peel (A flat piece of wood that holds the loaves of dough to place into the oven and remove the baked bread.)

Well, the big moment had arrived, and we placed the bread in the oven and waited like expectant fathers to see the results. The resulting product was in the strictest sense a success, for it was palatable and adequate to sustain life. The exterior of the loaf was rather black, which we expected, and the crumb was a little heavier than the text-book variety. But if soldiers were coming through that day and needed to be fed, we would have been able to feed them even under the worst circumstances.

BASIC TRAINING NEARLY COMPLETE

We are now nearing the end of our training period, and whereas no one received grades as in a regular classroom, the grading period will reflect in the issuing of various grades of ranks. In our spare time and when we were given a pass, we would go out on the town. Before this could happen, we had to know our general orders by memory. These were a series of rules applicable to army code, and it was mandatory to know them and recite them before the pass was given.

This one time, it would have been better than I would have missed on the orders. A bunch of guys and myself went out on the weekend to Richmond, Virginia. We bought some liquor and decided to have a party in our rented room. One of the whiskeys was Rye whiskey, which I thought would be fun to try. The initial effects were pleasant and satisfying, but I learned a valuable lesson that day that more than doesn't make it better.

As I continued to drink (at age 22), the poison, which alcohol is listed as clinically, wasn't being passed out of my system fast enough. As a result, I went into stages of vomiting that lasted a long time and took all the fun out of the weekend. I mention this because I was young, inexperienced, and much later in life became an alcoholic. I will cover this more extensively in later chapters.

The expected day for our graduation had finally come. An air of expectancy and apprehension stimulated everyone. I, for my part, really didn't know what to expect. There were ratings to be had because we were being trained to become cadre and train other units. The day finally came, and ratings were being awarded in alphabetical order, which put me down the list and, of course, added to my impatience. I could see the ratings being given out. There were many private first class and a goodly number of corporal ratings and occasionally a sergeant rating. This sergeant rating was usually the T-sergeant, which stood for a technician. It applied to the job the person would perform and was not related to the training of men or authority over them, except men assigned to him of lower rank. His stripes consisted of three stripes and a "T" on the bottom, and honestly, I never held high regard for a "T" rating, and I really don't know why perhaps because all of my superiors had regular stripes and carried the weight of authority.

They were getting down in the alphabet now, and soon I would know the fruits of my efforts. My thoughts were in the line of corporal, and I felt I'd be satisfied with that since that is a jump of two ranks, which isn't bad. Suddenly, I heard my name shoot out with a knife-like piercing resonance, my pulse quickened, and my blood ran hot. Paradoxically a chill ran through me as I made my way forward. I could see the officer holding Staff Sergeant stripes, and I couldn't conceive that they were for me! This became a reality with alarming swiftness since here he was handing the stripes to me and affirming it with "Congratulations, sergeant!" Taking the stripes without hesitation, I stepped back and saluted and offered an excited "Thank you!" After we were dismissed, the impact really hadn't taken effect and had to work its way through the euphoric daze I was in.

This was unbelievable since it isn't feasible for a person to move from private to four ranks up, sergeant and staff at that! There weren't many of those ratings given out, and I was truly flattered that this happened to me. At the barracks, the men I had been living with these past months looked askance as they were fully aware of my promotion. There was no wasted time on my part on letting them know I was still the same guy and wanted to be their friend.

This problem or near problem was solved rather uniquely when we all ended up in the men's latrine and started to shoot dice. The game was rolling along and escalating with high stakes and perhaps twenty to twenty-five men participating. The game in progress was halted abruptly when a staff sergeant came in, told everyone this was against regulations, and everyone was going on report. I was standing in the back out of sight, but my stripes were already sewn on my shirt. I stepped out in plain sight and said, "Just a minute, sergeant, these men are under my authority and under my supervision; I take full responsibility for their actions."

The look on his face couldn't be duplicated even if he had hit a million-dollar lottery. He didn't say a word but spun around briskly on his pivot heel and melted out of sight. We heard no more about this, and my friends were elated over the incident and made me feel like a hero. This was very rewarding, and it dawned on me the impact the rating can generate. I was careful not to misuse my rank since I didn't want to lose the stripes as fast as I got them. Too, I had resolved to be a good sergeant who would be fair but firm.

The time was drawing near for our departure. All the friends I'd made would be separated again, and we would be off in different directions with destinations unknown. Leaving Camp Lee didn't devastate me, but to leave new-found friends leaves the nostalgia in a tattered condition. To leave Virginia, with its special kind of crud, wasn't hard to deal with. You see, we were camped on an area that looked like lake sand in these tents that held six, and in a short while, all the men developed this crud that manifested itself in chronic coughing and expectorating a yellowish type of sputum. Even the native Virginians acknowledge this to be so.

DEPARTURE FROM CAMP LEE

When the day came for our departure, there were many sad good-byes. I learned through channels that I was headed to the state of Oregon. This news was hearsay, of course, because logic would dictate that you just don't go three thousand miles away. Still, as I learned later, these are tactics used to confuse the enemy, whose spies lurked secretly, picking up bits of information to relay to the main headquarters to help their strategy.

Many of us boarded the train, which were sleepers or, as we called them, Pullmans. The seats could be adjusted into beds, and there was also an overhead compartment that pulled down, which formed an upper bunk. The beds were comfortable and had clean sheets; we appreciated this more and more as our train ride lasted at least five days. The realization of the vastness of our country becomes a reality when crossing it becomes an actuality. Part of the route took us through North and South Dakota, Montana, Nebraska, Utah, and Wisconsin. There were many sights, and the beauty of the varying topography was engulfingly enhancing. At this time of year, the cold weather was about to set in up North, yet it was still mild back in Virginia.

OREGON

Wow, that was quite a time lapse between my last page of my account of my life May 10th, 1986, and now, July 20, 2000.

And now, I have the new impetus, however, since I have new hope that my efforts have not been in vain. So, I will continue from the point where I left off.

We took the train cross-country to our destination, Oregon. The journey itself disclosed various parts of these United States as we viewed rolling hills, farmlands, lush grass, cowboy country, mountain ranges, and even semi barren areas. However, the most outstanding memories are centered in our passing through the Rocky Mountains, which really are properly named. The route, in a sense, is treacherous since the train circles the mountain in its climb. This effort requires two engines since the ascent is steep. As we were coming out of the Rockies, I was treated to a dramatic moment that took my breath away.

As we made the final turn, the Columbia River was suddenly to our right. I gazed on the other side of the river and viewed an artistic scheme that I would not believe if I hadn't seen it myself. There, right before me, the sands of the river were in various shades of muted colors, spectacular in their softness and beautiful to the point of being unreal. In years past, I had seen paintings similar to that and always felt that the artist had a wild and fantastic imagination. Now, here it was right in front of me. Thank God!

Soon, we passed through Salt Lake City, and the reception there was just wonderful. One aspect of that city that I wish to mention is the way they took the salt out of the lake. This method was simple enough. When the tide came in, they blocked certain portions from receding. The sun-dried out this water, and a white residue of salt was left.

Our journey ended up in Portland, Oregon. It is important to mention that Oregon is really a beautiful state. Portland is near the city of Vancouver and right near the Canadian border. If my memory does not fail me, there is a Vancouver, Washington, and a Vancouver, British Columbia, Canada. You see, Portland borders the state of Washington. Our stay in Oregon covered a few months, so being a young man of 22 or so, I dated a young lady in Portland named Frances Morris. About the same time, I met a very pretty school teacher in Vancouver. A peculiar situation developed out of this arrangement, which is worth recounting.

I had a date with the girl in Vancouver, but that day I checked the bulletin board and found that I was on duty as sergeant-of-the-guard at that same time. I called Vancouver and explained my situation to the young lady. She said she understood. In the meantime, another sergeant friend of mine, Sol Sherwin, said he would take my place as sergeant-of-the-guard, so

I jumped at the chance.

I'd broken off my date in Vancouver, and I couldn't reach her when I called back, so I called a girl in Portland and got a date. At that time, they had service clubs for servicemen called USO's. My Portland date and I went to one of these clubs in Vancouver! We danced, and as we danced, I turned and was brought face to face with my broken date from Vancouver. I said I could explain, but she said, "forget it," which is the last I saw of her.

From here, our group moved across the United States to a jumping-off place on our way to going overseas. Just before that, we had a ten-day furlough. I went home, but travel time ate up eight days of the ten. From Indiantown Gap (Pennsylvania), we moved to New Jersey for the final step of our going overseas. They had a procedure they called "shakedown." This involved going through all your clothing, and even if it is slightly worn, you throw it out on a big pile in the middle of the street. This procedure is a tribute to the productivity of the U.S. economy. When I first got drafted, we were ill-prepared. We had no guns and trained with *broomsticks*.

TROOPS SHIP ACROSS THE ATLANTIC OCEAN

The day of departure came, and it was an awesome sight with thousands of soldiers entering the troopships to face the hazards of war. These hazards were also reflected in the unsafe conditions of the Atlantic Ocean, with submarines lurking at a chance to strike. However, we didn't go unprotected since we had two battleship escorts, cruisers, and many destroyers. The convoy was huge and stretched out as far as I could see. Nevertheless, the threat was still there, and we knew we weren't going on a picnic. However, the mood of young guys takes more than that to shake the morale since the cause was on our side, and we are on our way to defend the country we love! There was a need to add here that I was patriotic, but I wasn't crazy!

The ship we were on was called an LST. We determined that this was short for the longer version "Long SLOW Target!" for the ship would look like a sitting duck to a submarine that had it in its sights. The journey lasted ten days, and during those days, we saw nothing but dark blue water with its crisp whitecaps bursting all around. Those ten days were uneventful, but there was some anticipation in realizing the situation. Yet, I am amazed at myself that I felt no real fear.

We were given our cots below, and I found mine was located against the ship's side. I looked at the wall and calculated that if a torpedo came in, it would land directly in my lap. We had instructions to follow, and one was that when the warning sirens went off, we were to go on deck. One night at 4:00 a.m., the siren went off. There was a mad rush to get up on deck, except me. I decided if it were real, I would take my lumps where I was at. After all, where do you go? It would be like changing seats on the Titanic. This alarm was a practice drill.

After ten days, we passed through the Strait of Gibraltar. This is between Sicily and the bottom toe of Italy. Before that, though, to enter the Mediterranean Sea, you must pass the Rock of Gibraltar. This is a huge precipice that is all rock and goes on and up forever, it seems. The British were stationed up whereas, they had a fortress guarding the entrance to the Sea. The ocean we were leaving was dark blue and still had the white caps and some turbulence. The Mediterranean, in contrast, was like riding on polished glass. The color of the water was a light turquoise and enhanced by its white-sand beaches.

ORAN, NORTH AFRICA

Our destination was Oran, Africa, and in a short while, we entered the harbor. It was late afternoon, still light, and we thought we would disembark in daylight. The army seems to have a slogan, however, that says "hurry up to wait," and this was no exception. After several hours of waiting, we loaded up with a full field pack, helmet, weapons, and barracks bag. We all were loaded on trucks and told we were on our way to where we would live. The night was pitch black. We were weary and exhausted and found hope that we would soon be in an established camp to bed down. As we drove along, the rain came and came, it was in sheets and torrents, and we got entirely soaked in an open truck.

ARRIVED AT THE CAMP

After driving around for what seemed for hours, the truck stopped by an olive grove. Through the darkness and the rain, we made out a grove of trees. The driver got out and stated, "This is where you live!" We said,

"Where?" He said, "HERE!" So we had to set up our pup tents in this grove and make camp. We did. The soil was like cement and hard to drive a peg into, so hard in fact that the helmets we used as a hammer dented in. After pitching a tent, we placed our raincoats on the ground inside the tent. We then laid our blankets on the raincoat as a mattress and had extra blankets to cover. When I say "we," I refer to two who share the same tent. Each man carries with him a half of tent which fit together as a whole tent. Then we each have a blanket, each made of 100% wool. We went to sleep, and that was the best sleep I ever had. The next morning, I woke up feeling great! Boy, it was good to be young!

MOVED TO ANOTHER CAMP

We later moved to a new location, an open area with about four or four inches of dust on the surface. They said it was the dry season and that the dust was dried out clay. The drawback was that we slept on the ground right in that dust. That was standard for the course, but for added spice, this dust was full of chiggers! This was an insect that not only bit you but dug his way into and under the skin. We had to sprinkle a special powder on the ground to prevent this. That's the way wars go, though, so it was no big thing.

The army trained me to be an army baker; we were good at it and baked thousands of pounds of bread. We waited for our equipment to come in, for it always took longer. This included portable ovens and all things necessary for field baking. These ovens came in crates and were reinforced with tough metal straps. When we went out to take them out of the crates, I had other ideas, and being a sergeant, the men I took with me were instructed to separate good lumber to one side and usable strapping along with nails that could be salvaged.

They wanted to know why, but I wouldn't tell them until later, and they saw why. When I saw lumber, I knew I could build a bed—off the ground—the straps made good springs, so the bed had "give." I filled my mattress cover with clean, dried grass for a mattress and had a bed fit for a king! Soon, all of the scrap lumber disappeared, and the strapping; that was the best clean-up job I ever saw.

After some time, we moved again. Going across Northern Africa, we passed areas where the war had been. The evidence was all around with pieces of tanks, planes, and bomb craters telling their own tale!

FROM ALGERIA TO TUNISIA

They moved the troops by train, but these trains were unlike the trains we got to know in the U.S. The trains had less power, much less. The boxcars we traveled in were French design and built to carry 40 men or eight horses. They were known as "40 & 8" cars. When we traveled, at the time, the train would run into an incline and couldn't get up the hill. The soldiers would jump down and start to push the train up the hill.

When we moved from Oran, which I believe is in the country of Algeria, we went to Tunis, Tunisia. There were other short layovers in between, but it would be too tedious to mention them all. Too, my memory escapes me in many areas.

We set up our bakery facilities in Tunis and baked bread for the troops that passed through on their way into combat. One particular day, a civilian and, as I later learned, a White Russian (a loose confederation of anti-communist forces that fought the communist Bolsheviks (Reds) came to us to see if he could get some bread. I talked to him and found a broken loaf, or I broke it to stay within the army regulations if it wasn't. This led to a friendship that had me become a daily visitor to his home in the evening after work. Good fortune smiled at me, and the man had a very attractive daughter in my age bracket, and we spent many pleasant evenings together.

Her name was Olga, and as luck would have it, after a certain time, she said she was in love with me. This is an undesirable situation for a soldier on the move and in a war. Somewhere, while in Tunis, I developed a case of the hives. These miserable things really drive you nuts. I had to go on a sick call, and the doctor didn't have the right medicine. So he said he would give me a shot of adrenalin. He told me to lie real still, for my heart would go fast and pound. The hives disappeared as if by magic never to return. He said they might, but they didn't. Thank God!

TUNISIA

While we were in Tunis, which incidentally all these people are Arabs, I heard about the Kasbah. This is a city within a city inhabited only by Arabs, it seems. There was a mystery connected to it in my mind that was enhanced by the fact the army warned us to keep it out because it was not considered safe. Anyway, this is the way I heard it. For that matter, the whole city wasn't safe, and the Arabs were regarded as untrustworthy and should be watched with suspicion and caution.

KASBAH

My curiosity burned within me, and I tried to get a couple of other soldiers to go in with me. I had no luck in this area. So, you can guess that I tried it myself. As I stood by the entrance, I saw crowds of Arabs inside milling around. I saw a very pretty woman walk into the Kasbah, and I followed her in. She got lost in the crowd in a hurry, but by this time, I was inside and decided to look around.

The streets were decidedly narrow, uneven on the surface, and were identical to the old-fashioned cobblestone. It crossed my mind that anyone living on one side of the street could reach out with effort and shake hands across the street with their neighbor. This may be a slight exaggeration, but it is pretty close to accurate. They worship Muhamad in the Arab world, so each door has a brass hand on it, and it is said to represent the hand of Fatimah, the daughter of Muhamad.

This is what I remember, but I suggest you look that up to verify it, for I am taxing a memory: just about 60 years removed from that scene. While there, I stopped in a shop that sold perfume, rugs, etc. What caught my attention was a beautiful camel hair rug in right tan, brown, white, and very dark brown colored stripes. The rug was about 15 feet long by 8 feet wide and cost $10 American money.

I would have bought it ordinarily, but there was a war on, and shipping was non-existent. While there, I bought a small vial of the essence of the perfume Shalimar. (Still one of the best-selling perfumes ever) The cost was one dollar and fifty cents (four hours wages from my old job). And from this, there was enough power to make a gallon of perfume. Later at camp, I needed money and sold the essence for $10. I regretted it, of course, but money at times became as scared as hen's teeth.

The journey continued as the hour of three in the afternoon approached. To my surprise, when 3 o'clock arrived, all activity stopped, and the Arabs went to the ground face down, facing east, and prayed. Being outnumbered by overwhelming odds, there was a snap decision on my part to join them, and I was down on my knees too, face down, facing east. That was not the time to make any enemies because I was right amid all these Arabs!

Shortly after that, I was about to witness an event that I would consider extraordinary in my wanderings! I have never heard of it EVER being mentioned in all my days. In my travels, I must have been very close to the center of this inner city. As I turned a corner, a large band of musicians situated on the side of the road came into view. They were dressed in their very best band uniforms and their instruments, mainly a trumpet type instrument, but very long, were polished to a high golden intensity, that was enhanced by the sunlight which caused glitters and gold flashes, sparkles. Further up the road from them, about a hundred and fifty feet, was an old type carriage replete in splendor, full of embellishments that seemed fit for a king.

While observing this, my good fortune was to find a good vantage point and yet be out of the way of everyone. I wasn't too positive that I was welcome at this celebration, so I tried to be obscure! Further up the road, I saw a black Cadillac (an American luxury car in Tunisia) driving up, and it stopped just in front of the carriage. A man got out dressed in royal clothes and entered the carriage. I failed to mention that the carriage had six beautiful horses, all white, spirited, and eager. The driver of the carriage, on command, drove a short way right in front of an ornate building, which I was to learn later was a palace.

Upon investigation, I learned that the man was a king but known in the Arab language as the "Bey of Tunis," a provincial governor of the Ottoman Empire, Muhammad VIII al-Amin. He would make periodic visits to the palace and have audiences with the people. So I was fortunate enough to see such an event, and shortly after, I didn't push my luck and got out of there.

PROCUREMENT

We were camped in an area and told that we could be there for a while. We lived in six-man tents and decided to make them more livable. Our officers agreed with this idea, but they also knew that the supplies were virtually impossible to get...supply sergeants again! There was a guard at the supply dump, and to get in, you needed a requisition for supplies and verification of need. We could type a requisition but had no verification.

I went to see the guard the day before and talked with him. I told him I was a baker, and I would be coming tomorrow for some supplies. I asked him if he and the other guards like American baked pies fresh out of the oven! The guard loved the idea. I told him I'd bring those pies the following day since I had to pick up some supplies. I also asked him if he would mind if we threw a few extra supplies on the truck, and he said he didn't mind. The next day my order form listed only one item: a keg of nails. When we pulled out of the yard, the truck was *loaded* to the top. We were happy so were the guards since they had their pies.

RAISIN JACK

An incident came back to mind, which I think will be of special interest. We had a detachment of men stationed near a city named Bizerte. (The northernmost city in Africa.) The whole city was just a bunch of rocks and rubble from heavy shell fire and bombs. Through this, the city only had a name but no inhabitants. This detachment of men, for some mysterious reason, was getting drunk and rowdy. Their production had fallen off, and the officer in charge was having difficulty with the men. For this reason, the lieutenant and I were sent up there to find out the cause of this disturbance. The drinking was the cause, but with no towns in the area, where did they get these potential libations? We did some slick detective work by following some of them into the rocky and wild countryside. There, in a well-secluded spot, was a mountain "still" set up behind some rocks! The bottom line was that they stole a box of raisins and sugar from the kitchen and made raisin Jack! (home-made wine made in the sun with raisins, grapes, water) We put an end to this and resumed regular army duties.

CLOSE CALL

The first one happened in Africa when we were quartered in tents. I already mentioned that we built our own beds, and not having any chairs, we sat upon our beds. Army regulations also required that our guns be kept clean and oiled. Our tent housed only Platoon Sergeants and the First Sergeant. I was sitting on my bed with my sub-machine gun in the process of cleaning it. Opposite me was another sergeant with his gun, and he was cleaning it. I noticed that there was a clip on it. A clip is a metal container that holds the bullets for the gun. The clip has a very strong spring in it and pushes another round into the chamber after the previous one has been fired. This is not allowed while cleaning a gun, and I mentioned this to the sergeant. He became indignant and said he wouldn't be stupid to have a loaded clip in the gun. A second later, a shot went right past my head and out through the tent roof! This was a 45 slug that would have blown my head off had it hit me! It didn't take long for the tent to fill up with officers and my captain leading the way. He wanted to know what happened, and I would not talk about it but said, "ask him, the guy who fired the shot." I don't know what happened after that!

AFRICA
Story spans 1943-1945 War & Discharge

I recall another incident in Africa that got my attention. It was an event that I couldn't possibly imagine, and had anyone told me they saw this, I would say it was made up, or their imaginations were wild and out of control! You see, what I am about to report is something I read about in the Bible, the Old Testament. It seemed to be a fable of exaggeration or a myth and was being used only as an example of Biblical truth. Let me relate the event as it happened and as I saw it and lived it.

While in the army, it seemed that I was always going somewhere with my lieutenant. This time, we had to go somewhere, but the name escapes me. It seems to me that it was in Algeria. We did travel a great distance and ended up in a well-populated city with Arabs scurrying here and there. They were dressed in robes and turbans, and the women were in veils. We felt out of place under those circumstances, but I must say the setting was very interesting. Toward the end of the day, it appeared that that light of the day diminished very suddenly. Then I glanced toward the west, and the skies became very dark, darker than I have EVER seen it. It seemed that a severe storm was on the way! The surprise that soon arrived was indeed a thing I will never witness again.

There had to be billions of locusts that flew in. They fell on the sidewalks, the streets, our eyes, all over us, in fact, and as we walked, it was like walking on popcorn or Rice Krispies with their snap, crackle, and pop. We made a hasty exit of that town in our Jeep, splattered windshield full of squashed locust and observing the foliage of surrounding trees disappear! Through this, I realized what the Bible talked about when it mentioned this type of infestation. Much of this can be found in the Book of Exodus. Too, John the Baptist lived on honey and locusts. Incidentally, when the locusts fell on the ground, the Arabs reached down, picked up a locust or two, pulled off its wings, and ate it!

CONSTANTINE

Sometime later, my lieutenant told me that we needed to go to the city of Constantine, the capital of eastern Algeria. Another man and I would accompany the officer on the way. The other man's name was John Reid. This was in June of 1943, summertime in Africa, which used to get quite hot. 100-degree temperatures were not uncommon. Yet, for reasons we didn't understand, we were told to take winter gear, including the heavy overcoats.

We started out with the spirit of adventure and drove until we reached a mountain range. The climb up the mountain was gradual, but as we drove, it appeared to get cooler. At first, it didn't tax much of my attention, but as it got colder and colder, the chill in my bones verified the fact. Then, a snowflake appeared, then two, and suddenly millions swirled around with authority. The road started to turn white but still very possible. This was to end since some American soldiers who were stationed up in those hills told us there were at least four feet of snow ahead, and the road was out.

We went to their camp that night, ate, and bedded down. Now we had no other option but to turn back and go home! On the way back, we had motor trouble, and the Jeep we were in stopped running. Here we are, stuck in the middle of nowhere, stranded. The lieutenant ordered John and me to go for help. The night was soon to fall, but we started out, of course. We had our guns with us. That country and the people were suspect.

The area we were in was wild and not settled at all; the possibility of wild animals could not be ruled out. We walked all night through those wild hills. John Reid, my companion, was good company, and we had fun in a sense, since what other options did we have? So here we are stuck out somewhere in Morocco, Africa. We walked all night and watched morning break. At about this time, we came out of the mountains and saw flat lands ahead.

The road we were on ran right ahead like a ribbon. We noticed that way down the road; there were 15 to 20 Arabs together. This looked dangerous to us, so when we got closer, I fired a 30-caliber shell over their heads. The crowd disappeared in a hurry, and perhaps they are still talking about it. The outcome is that we did get help through all that effort. All things change, and we had orders to move out of Africa. Olga, the White Russian, was shattered, but war is war.

ITALY

We boarded an English wooden ship run by a crew from India. We passed through the Straits of Messina, with Sicily to the left and Italy to the right (Editor's note: narrow strait also connects the Tyrrhenian Sea to the north with the Ionian Sea to the south within the central Mediterranean.) We landed in Anzio (southern Italy), which had been a real hot spot with very intense fighting and heavy casualties (wounded). It was not safe as yet, for we had to watch out for mines and some trigger-happy soldiers. Not too far from there, we saw rows and rows of graves dug, ready and waiting. Close by; there were bodies of dead American soldiers lying around to be buried. This was the reality of war in its brutal grimness.

I was in charge of a detail to dig a sump pit (a pit for refuse, etc.) There was a big problem; the spot we were digging in was solid clay. We made little progress and were on limited time. We just started a new camp due to our frequent moves. It was to confuse the enemy, so they were never certain of our location. One guy suggested we use dynamite, a stick at a time, to loosen the clay. I thought it was a good suggestion, and we did. We started out with one stick at a time with poor results. (A stick of dynamite is like a firecracker, a large one. It is close to 10 to 12" long and about an inch and a quarter thick.) We would pound out a round hole into which the explosive fit and set it off with a long fuse (giving us time to take cover).

Since we had poor results with one stick, we added another stick and then another until we were up to ten sticks at once. This time the results were TOO good, and it blew a hole in the ground and sent chunks of clay flying all over. One baseball-sized piece fell right through the officer's tent and hit their table. They happened to be having their supper at the moment. That ended the dynamiting and my ears rung for weeks from the officer's rage! They couldn't punish me for it all happened in the line of duty.

One more incident I'll report happened in Italy right after we landed in Anzio. The battle zone (battle Jan-June 1944) isn't a desirable place to be; it makes everyone alert and keeps a soldier on edge. It was standard to have a guard posted at places of importance, and I was out in that area with a large field, and in the distance, I saw an American soldier on guard. As I was crossing the field, this trigger-happy guard took a shot at me. His rifle dispatched a 39-caliber shell my way that whistled on its way by. It wasn't "whistling Dixie" either. I hit and ground and discovered that I could crawl on my belly for long distances….and fast too!

Our layover in Anzio was short, but circumstances prevailed that allowed me to see Naples and Rome. The Vatican is a story in itself with its fine art and beautiful buildings. St. Peter's dome is truly a masterpiece and really deceptive as to its height and size. I saw the Swiss guards and stood at the tomb of St. Peter himself. This was really awesome since he was the first Pope and knew and lived with Jesus.

My memory has faded as to some events, but I do recall one event that is burned in my memory. John Reid and I went into Naples. It so happened that John was a light-fingered artist. He told me that I should watch him closely when we go into a jewelry store as he steals a ring. He told me very assuredly, that even if I watched, I could not defect it. So, he stole the ring, and I never saw it, but the jeweler wasn't fooled since there was a ring missing off the jeweler's board. This guy called the MP on ME. You can be sure that I took care of John Reid when I got to camp!

Let us move on to my next move courtesy of the United States Army. When we landed in Africa and Italy, we entered the port of that country. This time we boarded an invasion vessel and conducted a full-size invasion. It may have been that the war was still close and in France, and if we landed the conventional way, in the harbor, we could be open from a raid by bombers. So, we became an invasion force. We had to climb over the side of the ship, which seemed a mile high, down a rope ladder in squares and dropped into a **Higgins boat**. This boat is specially made for invasions.

It is really sad, but before this boat was invented, we lost many of our boys in previous invasions. The boat has high protective sides and hits the beach as the front falls forward to form a bridge onto the beach. (used for amphibious landings). The soldier then runs forward in the attack mode. We crawled down into the boats, and the anticipation was there. However, there was no resistance, so we are credited with the invasion of SOUTHERN FRANCE, not NORTHERN FRANCE! The area we landed on was a long beach with a wooded area about 200 feet ahead. We got credit for this on our discharge status since the invasion counted for one battle star. Confused?

Each battle we engaged in was worth one star. I had three battle stars. So, when we were getting discharged, it all depended on the time of service, foreign service, and battles. All other stuff was worth one point, overseas 2 points (This is by the month), and battle stars each were worth three points each. So, my total point amounted to 73 points, which resulted in my discharge in a more reasonable time.

INVASION 1944

You see, the whole world was expecting the invasion of Northern France, but it was imperative that it should be a matter of extreme secrecy! Thousands upon thousands of lives depended on this, and a leak would have been disastrous. This leads me to the account I am about to describe.

One morning, I was sent into a town in Italy. The nature of the business escapes my mind. There was a dramatic change this morning. The town was flooded with troops, trucks all over, ships in the harbor, and other equipment items in large quantities. I have seen soldiers in town before and military equipment too, but in this quantity, it was something that couldn't be ignored. I didn't ask any questions, finished my business, and went back to camp.

The next day I had to go to the same town and was in for another shocking surprise! As loaded as it was before, it *was totally deserted* and had the appearance of a ghost town. When I got back to camp, I told everyone I thought the invasion was about to begin. They doubted it and took what I said lightly. The next day they had the proof, I was one of the few who knew it the day before!

The following day was D-Day.

FRANCE

We entered France and ended up at the Port of Marseille, where we bunked in several places during our stay. Some interesting and unusual things happened here that I feel will be worth mentioning. First, the lieutenant and I and John Reid were driving along the beach of Southern France. I should mention that John was a buck sergeant, that is, three stripes. As we drove along the beach, the surrounding countryside was too pretty to ignore with the dense foliage covering the hillside, accented by scattered red-roofed homes! As we drove along the shore of the Mediterranean Sea and drinking in the beautiful wonders of nature, we came upon a clearing that led right to the shoreline. This part of the beach was about 125 to 150 feet wide. The shore was broken up by various size stones lying around, but there was enough clearing for a rowboat to make a landing.

Someone had tried this too; there was an American rowboat lying on its side, a body lying next to it. Across the whole clearing by the road was a chain stretched across with a sign in German: Achtung MINEN! We stopped the Jeep to take a look! The lieutenant then said the dumbest thing I have ever heard. "See who that is," he said. Now orders have to be followed, but this was ridiculous. I told John to follow me. That 100 or 150 feet was the longest trip I have ever made; each step could have been my last. We identified the man by his dog tags, which read, "John Larior, U.S. Navy from California. There was a bullet hole through his chest, and the body was preserved by the saltwater and had no odor. We called the Navy, and they took care of the matter.

CAMP

At one time, we were camped in a former boys' school. It had been run down since the war had put a stop to all activity, repairs, etc., and totally disrupted life as we generally consider normal. Since we were to live there for a while, we decided to fix it up for ourselves so it would be more livable. There were plenty of rooms there, and the men had good accommodations. Since I was an officer, I always had a private room.

During a war, there are always some soldiers who get captured and become prisoners of war. This war was no exception, so we had our share of prisoners. To clarify this, we as an outfit had no prisoners, but there were prisoners in prison camps that would be sent to us to work. They sent them to me and in my charge.

GERMAN PRISONERS

One morning they sent me about twenty prisoners to put to work. They were standing in the yard when I arrived that morning, and when I arrived in their presence, they all snapped to attention, clicking their heels, and saluted me. Man! I thought, how well trained can you get? And I returned their salute. They were put to work at various tasks in an area that was very large and needed attention. At the way back of this former boys' school was a large swimming pool that badly needed attention. I sent five or six Nazis in there to scrape the walls and prepare for a new paint job. I don't speak German, but I can speak Polish, and one German knew Polish.

It happened to be a Sunday, and he asked me why they had to work on Sunday. This was an audacious remark for a prisoner and especially for a German, and it irritated me. So, I told him not to ask me. You better ask Adolph Hitler. My guard understood Polish too, so I told him in Polish to keep an eye on these prisoners and especially this one, and if he stops working even for a second, shoot him in the head. That sounds terrible, but it was for the German, not us. Then I got the guard aside and told him that we are civilized human beings and not like the Nazis, so he knew we don't do things like that.

The guard told me later that the prisoners never stopped working. When they had finished cleaning the pool out, I had them paint it. Choice of color was no problem since the army only used one color...Green! Then there was a problem with how to fill it, but I saw a clear stream running in the back of the lot. I got a long hose, dropped it into the stream. Then on the other end, I drew on it with some very deep gulps. The results were amazing; the water began to pour out and right into the pool! This pool had to be at least fifty feet long and twenty feet wide, and ten feet deep on the deep end! The men appreciated it!

The captain called me into the office one day and said he needed a man to teach a class called "Information and Education." He said that he had selected me for this job. To understand the army, you must know that when your superior officer says YOU will do this...YOU DO IT! This task then needed training in teaching techniques, and I was sent to school. They sent me to the University of Paris for this training.

When I arrived, I was shocked to find only officers there and felt uneasy in this fast company. Nevertheless, I survived, came back, holding classes, and completed my mission. There was another class I conducted on the subject of baking. We had to teach the men both the technical and practical aspects of baking. This class included some simple chemistry and explaining how and why things worked s they did. These classes were always two hours long, and we had to know our stuff.

BAKING AND FRENCH BAKERS

Once again, but sometime later, the captain called me into his office and said I needed a rest, and he was going to send me to Nice, France on the Riviera! (story to follow) We had requisitioned a large bakery in France under the Marshall Plan. (economic redevelopment) This plan was meant to help out the people in France since the war had hurt their economy.

The bakery we ran was very large and had six large ovens. We mixed doughs that weight 750 pounds for each mix and produced 96,000 pounds of bread every twenty-four hours! The plan was to employ French workers under American supervision to help their employment situation.

I was in charge of the whole operation and the main trouble-shooter. In other words, if anything went wrong, I was supposed to know the answer. The French workers were pro-Communists and had a very strong union. In other words, they had every small job broken down into categories that they only did a certain thing. To be a baker, you must perform MANY functions from rolling bread, mixing bread, making loaves, putting in pans, putting in the oven, and baking. The sergeant that I designated to oversee this operation couldn't get the workers to do other operations.

We were late and falling behind, so in his anger, he fired the whole crew...at four in the morning. This was with a floor full of raising doughs and ovens full of bread. We needed help desperately! So, I rehired the workers, and they went back to work. I explained to my sergeant the urgency of the situation, but I would stand behind him. That morning, when the shift was over, I got all of the workers in the outer office and told them they would follow our rules or don't show up tonight. I said, there are soldiers who will take your place! That night, they all showed up!

FRENCH RIVIERA VACATION– POOR ME!

To anyone who is not familiar with the Riviera, this has always been a popular vacation area for affluent people worldwide. Movie stars and other people of world-renown have gone there for years. Nice is located right on the Mediterranean Sea; its hotels are built on the shoreline overlooking the sea. They were all exclusive places with all the fineries the human mind could imagine. Along the entire beach was an area that was a walkway called the "Promenade des Anglais." There were beach chairs and sofas to relax on after a fine swim of the Med. We stayed at a hotel called "The Nigresco," and it was an unforgettable experience. (Editor's note: hotel part of a chain, and this posh hotel still exists today 2020 although constructed in 1912) Our party was only about three, and we were treated to clean sheets and served dinner in the fancy dining room. This is a memory that will always remain in my memory.

JEWISH FRIEND

My army induction introduced me to a random cross-section of people that I would otherwise have not met. Mainly, most were Ohio boys, but there were others from various parts of the country. Each came from a particular walk of life, and each had his own specific trade to gain a livelihood. One of these fellows was from Cleveland, a Jewish fellow, who was part owner of the Sherwin Bakery Company.

Since he was a sergeant of the same rank as I, we were thrown into close proximity and ended up being part of the same company. We each had charge of one platoon; mine was the second platoon, and his the third. Sergeants of our rank shared the same quarters, along with the first sergeant. The Jewish fellow's name was Sol Sherwin, and we got to be very good friends. We were never in conflict, never had an argument, and confided in one another. It was my deepest feeling within that if he was in danger on the battlefield, I would crawl out to help him even if it meant my life was in danger!

This view is a radical turnabout from my previous conceptions since I grew up with extremely biased and segregated ideas. Society, at that time, embraced the ideas of prejudice toward other races. Poles were polaks,

139

Hungarians were hunkies, Jews were kikes, Italians were wops, and each race had a derogatory name ascribed to it.

I heard these things in my home and grew up with them. This is all my parents knew: all of society believed. This is no condemnation of their attitude, for this is what was passed on to them. You can understand then that when Sol and I came home on leave, I had him come to my home. I didn't know what manner of reception he would receive. Dad and Mom were very gracious, which showed their true character.

There was more to come later since Sol was to be married after discharge and asked me to be in his wedding party. I accepted without hesitation. At this time, this went against the norms. Yet my conscience told me otherwise. The wedding was in Cincinnati. My cousin Stan and I went together, got a hotel room, and attended the wedding. I stood up for Sol, wore that little black beanie the Jews wore, and still have it as a memento! The wedding was a good learning experience for me since my attitudes had a complete reversal.

Jews are not stingy; they are generous, care about others, are intelligent, they can hurt, enjoy, grieve, and are truly human. So, I find that all of life is a school for learning, and if we don't use it in that sense, we miss the purpose of life itself!

BE CAREFUL WHO YOU ASK TO BAKE A CAKE

Another incident worth mentioning happened either in Italy or France. We were trained as bakers of bread *only*, and that was our duty. Of course, we were bakers and could bake cakes, etc., but our job was to bake only bread. One day the lieutenant ordered us to bake a birthday cake for another officer. We told him that we only baked bread. The "we" in this case is my buddy and close friend, Sgt. Sherwin. He was part owner of the Sherwin Baking Company and Catering Service and was a very good baker. We were both furious at this officer for this order but said we would bake it and decorate it.

We got a detail of men to work for us as we mixed the batter for the cake. We had the men kill all the flies they could find and threw them into the cake batter. The cake baked fine, we decorated it, and it was truly a beautiful job. When we delivered it, the officer was delighted, but he didn't know what we knew. Sol and I joined a poker game with the first sergeant at the end of the hall; the party was at the opposite end. Sometime later, they must have cut the cake because right after that, I heard my name called out that really sounded like the crack of a rifle! Of course, I had to respond to this and knew what to expect.

He exploded when he said, "The cake was full of flies!" My response in the most innocent manner I could muster was, "Well, sanitary conditions in the kitchen were far from ideal, and I can see how a few flies could have fallen in the batter!" He shouted at the top of his lungs, "A FEW FLIES?" That cake was loaded with them! The incident resulted in a six-week confinement to the area, but I told him I didn't care for there was no place to go anyway. Of course, he blew up again! He had to depend on me, for I was his sergeant, and the only things he really knew about baking is what I would teach him. So, in a short time, he backed off, and we became "friends" again. Some of these things are not who I am now, and I have learned since then that to get even that was not the right way. I was 24 at that time, and today I smile at some of the stupid things I had done. Nevertheless, it must be told the way it was!

REFERENCE
TO THIS POINT IN TIME

Some facts that may be of interest: When the war broke out, we were just coming out of a Great Depression. When I finally got my job, my starting rate was forty cents an hour. After working three and a half years, my raises had raised my starting rate to 67 and one-half cents an hour. The shop's top rate was a dollar an hour, but you needed to be skilled labor to get that. The war escalated work and continued after the war. A glass of beer was a nickel. A cigar was a nickel; ice cream cones were a nickel; houses sold for $1,500, and a new car was $350 to $750. These are some facts worth mentioning. We had the mentality not to waste anything, and I also have never met a supply sergeant who didn't follow that rule. Even if we needed two batteries for our flashlights, he would give anyone a hard time over it. They were the same here in the states or overseas.

LONE GERMAN PRISONER

One day in Marseilles, France, I was standing in front of the bakery talking to my guard. Coming up the street on the opposite side was a German soldier! We were shocked to see this, and I sent my guard over to bring him in. I took him into my office and questioned him. He had wandered off from a work detail and had gotten this far. The guy was starved, so I fed him as much brad as he could eat and then called the military police (MPs), and they took him.

ITALIAN PRISONERS COOPERATED

We had Italian prisoners too, but we treated them differently since we didn't regard them as a threat. They all told us the same story that they were lovers, not fighters. We got along with them very well. Some of these soldiers were Alpine Troops that Mussolini was very proud of, the cream of the crop! They were all built like Charles Atlas (famous bodybuilder).

MORALE UNDER MY WATCH

Whenever we were camped way out in no man's land, I felt it was important to maintain morale with my own contribution toward this end. Consequently, I would end up in the kitchen baking either cookies, pies, or a large cake. We had plenty of help since I could appoint anyone to work without any backtalk. This is the way the army functions. They may have been well-trained soldiers, but they were still little boys at heart. When I made cookies, they were the easiest to steal—and they did, but I was happy that some were left to serve for supper. Cakes were too big to steal since they were made on a large sheet, then frosted with a boiled icing made of granulated sugar.

Boiling made a beautiful icing that had eye appeal and an appealing gloss. We applied it while very warm and liquid poured on, spread while hot, and left to cool, then it hardened. One day, I made a variety of fruit pies that had 9" tins, and this is a good-sized pie. After baking, I left the pies to cool. There must have been seven or eight pies when I left. When I came back, there were three left. One stolen pie wouldn't disturb me at all since if I were on the other side; I'd be the one doing the stealing.

Well, I was pretty disturbed about this but secretly flattered that, in a way, they were saying I was a good baker. Would they steal something if it wasn't appetizing? Nonetheless, I couldn't let this go undiscovered.

So, my inspection went from tent to tent. They could have eaten some of them, but I counted on at least finding one. The second to last tent I went to didn't disappoint me. To understand this, you should know that the tent was large enough to room six men and held six cots. At the entrance was a large flap that could cover the doorway opening. In good weather, it was folded up above the door, causing an inner flap. As I came to the opening, there was a definite sag in the flap. So I said," Well, I can't find anything," and at the same time, I reached up and tapped this hidden pie. As I was leaving, I warned them that bad things would happen to anyone caught stealing... and left.

They were good people, and we all were in the war together. Rarely was an order given that was disputed or challenged since this perverse action could generate severe consequences. Yet, there always is one bad apple in the barrel. I gave an order to a soldier, and he challenged me by saying, "You wouldn't be that tough if you didn't have those stripes!" I looked him in the eye as I slowly took my shirt off and said, "There are no more stripes to stand in the way, so let's go outside on even terms!" His attitude took an abrupt change as he hawed and hemmed. But I made my point and gained his respect.

BARBERSHOP

This may have been in Marseilles or Paris; I am not sure. We had opportunities to go into town, and on one of those occasions, I met a young man about my age. He was a Frenchman and very handsome, tall, and articulate. Barely will you hear another guy mention some other guy is handsome, but I got to tell the truth. This young man spoke to be in very good English, told me about himself, and said he was a member of the FFI. This abbreviation is short for Freedom Fighters of the Interior.

We talked for a while and joked around a bit, and then he asked me if I wanted to play a trick on some barbers. The plot was this: We would go into the barbershop, and each takes a chair. Then we would speak only English to each other, and while we were talking, he'd keep moving around in the chair while the barber was cutting his hair. He was doing this and relating to me the conversation of the angry barber to the other one cutting my hair. We tried not to laugh. When we were finished and had reached the door, my new friend turned to the barber and broke out in a rapid flurry of French that made the barber's chin drop. This had to be a mean trick, but we were young too, and it seemed funny at that time.

It still is, in a morbid sort of way!

GUNFIRE

Back in France in Marseilles, we occupied a building which had been a former date factory. It had a lot of space and a room large enough to house a large contingent of men with cots side by side. Occasionally, there would be a black-out for an air raid. While all was thoroughly black, in the darkness, these guys really surprised me. With bombers flying overhead, it seemed logical that they would be scared and seek cover. Instead, in utter blackness, they were having all types of arguments as they kept stealing each other's blankets!

In this same building was a room that was our kitchen. We would gather in the kitchen at night, drink coffee and talk. The kitchen was right next to the street and had a huge corrugated steel door. This door, when rolled up, was used for a truck unloading dock for our supplies. This particular evening, we were there as usual drinking coffee and talking when suddenly and without warning, a series of shots rang out right outside the door.

We scattered in a hurry, and I ran to get my weapon, which was a submachine gun. I was going to go outside, and the captain asked where I was going. Then he said, "Follow me!" We went out into the darkness and saw shooting down the road, about 150 feet. The captain had his pistol drawn, a 45 automatic, and as he ran forward, stumbled, and a shot went off! This drew a response from down the road as we saw the orange outburst of fire from their weapons. We ducked into a doorway by then, but I had a very strong urge to return their fire. In the army, you need permission, and the captain said, "Hold your fire!" We stayed quietly in the doorway until things got very quiet and then went back into the building.

Now, I being young and dumb, wanted action because I was good with my machine gun! This is not an idle statement; while we were in training, we periodically went to various ranges to monitor our skills. Well, there was a range for the submachine gun. This machine gun was the Thompson Sub-machine gun, to be more specific. The range was entirely different than a rifle range. On a rifle range, you remain immobile and shoot at a stationary target. This range of the target could be as far as 200 to 300 feet away. Not the machine gun range, for it is a measuring of reflex skills and promptness of reactions and their accuracy. The shooter is required to stand flat-footed facing unexposed targets.

The targets are spread out from one side to another. We are given 50 rounds with which to fire, and the course comes in two parts. One is a single shot; the second is a rapid-fire of three shots apiece. As the participant stands ready, a target will appear in the form of a man. It might be head and shoulders only, just the head, or a full figure. There is a time limit since the target appears for only so long. A single shot was comparatively easy since it doesn't require one shot, for the gun could be set that way. The second part was more difficult, for to dispatch three shots only, you barely touched the trigger. The top score of the course was 100. I hit every target but lost two points, and this is what happened: on the second last round, I squeezed off four shots instead of three.

This meant that there were only two bullets left for the last target. I hit that target too but lost two points over the one bullet that I had used up previously. This showing qualified me for a medal, the *expert* medal. My final score was 98 out of 100. It may sound now that I am feeding my own ego, but facts are facts. Out of the whole battalion, *I had the best score.* There are approximately six hundred men in a battalion, counting all the officers. Years later, I always felt that the army should have given me my due.

The expert medal is hard to come by, and I earned it. On occasions through the years, this thought would come to me about my medal. Many years had passed, perhaps fifty or so. (**Frank never received a physical medal/commendation while on active duty.**) One day I decided to pursue a solution to the problem. At that time, my U.S. Senator was Howard Metzenbaum (Ohio 1974, 1976-1995). He seemed to me to be a kind and caring man. So, I sat down one day, writing a letter in full detail. This was done mainly to satisfy me, and not expecting results for this would be a trivial matter to anyone else but me. To my surprise, I received a letter from the Senator that he would look into the matter. Later, there were letters detailing the progress of the investigation, until one day, a letter came and said all my records had been burnt in a St. Louis fire. They requested a copy of my discharge and pursued the completion of this discrepancy. Not too long later, I received not only my medal but medals I had due me. I have them to this day for anyone to see!

STARS AND STRIPES – MORALE BOOST

We had an army newspaper called the "Stars and Stripes." It kept us informed as to the way the war was going and good for the morale. There were days, though, that hope would leave, and it seemed like we would be there forever. We were camped out in the field one night in our pup tents. Our location was outside a French town. During the night, there was an air raid, and we had to run for cover. Well, this doesn't really add up to a restful night. When I awoke in the morning, I was very depressed, gutted when I opened my tent flap. In the sky, there before me was a huge gold cross ablaze by the bright rays of the morning sun! My depression lifted at once, for I knew now that God had not forgotten us. Oh, the cross was real, since somewhere in town was a Catholic Church with that cross on it when I went to investigate. Praise the Lord!

BACK TO CLEVELAND

The girlfriend in Rocky River really had my attention. Yet, I am the kind of person who studies the traits and honesty in one's make-up. We were on a double date one evening and ended up in a bar near her home. She and her girlfriend kept wandering off and visiting other people at the bar. This was undesirable at best, so we just got up and went home...without them. The next day she called and tried to make amends. That lack of quality did not appeal to me, so I ended it right there. This split was very difficult, but it was better to be sorry now than later.

My cousin Richard was dating a girl (Stephany) on the South Side in a strictly Polish neighborhood. I went along with him and became attracted to one of her sisters named Irene. We dated for some time, and then we were engaged. However, one evening, she let me know that she wasn't so sure of this engagement and returned my ring. The next day she changed her mind, but to me, that was it. She wanted to get back together again, but I felt it could happen again, so I refused to start over again.

There were other girls, too, but I won't pursue that since a lot of them were frivolous affairs without substance. There was one that I was engaged to, but she was of another religious belief. When she said that I would have to change to her church, that relationship ended.

REGRETS

Sometime after this, I stopped working in the bakery and was unemployed. The Powerlite Switchboard Co. invited me back to work there, but I needed a change. I ended up working for Higbee's, selling boys' clothing. I need to interject some thoughts here and make a point. Being a young man has its disadvantages as related to making the wrong decisions. I made a very bad one and let a wonderful opportunity slip through my fingers. Through an act of Congress, the veterans who had been discharged had been offered a free paid college education for four years. It was called the G.I. Bill of Rights.

This bill was a chance of a lifetime and would certainly enhance my earning power, yet I let it slip by. I thought I wasn't smart enough to do it, or lazy, or whatever, but it is now a deep regret. I regret, too, that I didn't learn to type when I had the chance, for I certainly could have used it now. I could have typed this instead of writing it, and I'm reminded of it with this sore thumb! Maybe this will be good advice to my grandchildren when and if they read this.

The job at Higbee's came about in this way. One afternoon I was downtown feeling like I was not a part of society. I wasn't doing anything, and that feeling of uselessness was taking over. Seeing Higbee's sign, I decided to step in and ask for a job. I applied for a job selling furniture, but the lady who interviewed me asked if I had any experience. Of course, I didn't, so she offered other options. I could see that she would give me a job, but it had to be one more suitable. She sent me to sell boys' clothes. It was a good job that paid salary and commission.

The salary was small, the commission tricky, and it ran monthly. This procedure made it difficult to make more money. The starting salary was $35 a week, but I got her up to $40 a week ($1 per hour). This increase raised my commission quota. I didn't care about that since "a bird in the hand is worth two in the bush!" My job here lasted until my father and brother approached me with the proposition: we should go into the bakery business together. My brother presented it in glowing terms and said we would become rich. Well, I never aspired to be ever "rich," just secure. I didn't want to do it on the one hand, yet a challenge beckoned on the other. My oldest brother, Walter, warned me not to do it since he said that John was hard to get along with. (John was the brother who asked me to be a partner.) Finally, I relented and said, "Yes!" This "yes" opened the door to many headaches, disagreements, and upset stomachs. There were good moments too, but in retrospect, the bad outweighed the good.

We made a living and paid all our bills, but we worked hard too and often under much stress. There was an alcohol problem and a very definite problem in communication. My father drank, and John went on periodic binges. When this happened, the bakery couldn't function, so we closed down. At this time, I was only a social drinker.

To put it in perspective, we lasted 17 or 18 years, which could be regarded as successful in the business sense. Too, there were ulcers and plenty of tension to go with it. The bakery was my living, though, an investment that my money was tied up in, and I had to stick with it! There were some light moments too, but the clash of personalities was a negative factor. I had many duties: frying donuts, rolling bread, making bread, working the oven, making pastry, doing the washings of pans, cleaning, bookkeeping, depositing bank deposits, delivering bread and pastry to stores for resale, cake decorating, and working in the store selling.

BAKERY CUSTOMER

I was attending the store, a mother and a young lady entered. The young lady caught my eye, for she had a vibrance and vigor about her as well as being very attractive. This evening visit happened a few times and stimulated my interest. One evening, the mother came in alone. I inquired as to the whereabouts of her daughter. Mother said she was at home, and if I wanted to see her, I could stop in. She gave me the full details of the address and specified that it was the upstairs apartment. You can be sure that I made haste to get there since this gal was stuck in my head.

The first time I went up to see her, we talked and learned about each other. The conversations were compatible and favorable. I learned that her father was doctoring but was capable of working. To describe him briefly would be to say he was of medium height, round face, but a face that could easily smile. He was in his fifties but still had a boyish look. He probably weighed about 160 pounds and was about 5' 9" or so.

This girl's name was Lola, but this was really a nickname, for her real name was Constance. The last name was Fedor which had been shortened from the Russian version "Fedorowitz." She was twenty years old, and I was thirty-one at the time. The disturbing thought came to me that I was too old for her, but I wanted to stick around anyway. I learned later that this wasn't even a factor. My activity at the onset was to try to help them out. The parents were older with many doctor visits and other duties which involved everyday activities. Yet, it made their life easier by my helping. Of course, this allowed me to be close to the young lady as my interest deepened. I was seeing her very often but with that certain uncertainty of my actual status in this relationship.

Apparently, this conjecture on my part was not one-sided. It all came to a head one afternoon on Roadway Avenue, near Anne's Vogue Bridal Shop. As we drove along, she asked me outright if I was her boyfriend or not?!? My feeble response was "yes" since in my long uncertainty of my status, to hear this was a shock of relief and left me limp. Now we could go further along, for I had direction. Sometime later, we discussed getting married. Her parents liked the idea too.

This was good since her father was very protective and possessive but seemed to trust me to do right by his daughter. I took this as a great compliment. These were very happy times, and Lola had a wonderful and generous personality. All other times, I wondered if I wanted to marry some of the women I dated, but this one left little doubt. We married in summer, but the exact date fails my memory. The church was St. John Nepomucene, with the blessing of Fr. Liederbach. You see, Lola was only baptized when she was sixteen, and Fr. Liederbach brought her into the church.

Next was the honeymoon, and we went to Mackinac (mac ken aw) Island, Michigan, for possibly two weeks. We had a wonderful time, and it remains a good thought in my memory. When we got back, I went back to work. We had agreed that she would stay away from the bakery to avoid complications. There were enough already with just my brother, John and myself.

NEWLYWED LIFE

We lived with my in-laws from the onset of this marriage to get a start in life. My father-in-law had bought a house on E. 71st Street for $7,000. He really didn't want to, he was content just to live on rent, but with my inducement, he bought the house. I paid room and board, which was helpful toward making payments on his house. Susan had been born while we lived on E. 71st Street. Lola followed the natural method of family planning, and one day she told me, "Today is my most fertile day," and I said, "Let's go for it!" Nine months later, Susan came onto the scene.

Of course, living together eventually causes friction (and even sooner than that at times), and we moved out to a rental of our own on Rathbone Avenue. We found upstairs rooms that were nice but drafty in the winter, but we were together and alone. Marilyn was born when we lived on Rathbone, and the time came early in the morning. We were in such a hurry that I smashed my finger in the car door. When Lola told me she was ready, with all the fuss, Susan awoke. She slept in a crib and wore red flannel pajamas with feet. Through all this, she stood up in her crib and said, "Me go too!" These are moments that are precious and last in the memory.

We took Susan to her grandmother's home. I went to the hospital with Lola. The hospital for both births was Grace Hospital (on W. 14th Street in the area known as "South Side.") In those days when you had a doctor, he did everything: delivery and anesthesia. Lola did not receive the ether well at all and always experienced vomiting after each delivery. When I came to see her, the room reeked from the smell of ether. After all, it is a form of alcohol with a lot of the water squeezed out of it. Anyway, we now have two girls and must look forward to larger quarters.

We had saved some money for a down payment and looked around. While riding on E. 53rd Street and Fleet, we passed this house that I still live in at 3822 E. 53rd St. Cleveland, Ohio 44105 (until his passing in 2009). There was a sign in the window that said "FOR SALE," so we stopped in. Lola liked the place, especially the kitchen. They were asking $13,500, and we would have taken it if we had a big enough down payment. Those days, a down payment of one-third was required. We only had $3,000, far short of the required amount. I told the owner that we would buy it, but the down payment was an obstacle. It now appeared the deal would never happen, only if they would lower the price to meet our down payment. A few weeks later, they called us and asked, "How's $10,500 sound?" I said, "FINE!" That is how we bought this home on E. 53rd Street.

A ROUGH SPOT

We moved in, and we accumulated funds for improvements; we made them except when Lola got impetuous and bought it anyway, on credit. I am opposed to credit on a regular basis, for it is like digging a hole with me in it. That hole can get very deep sometimes. I'd always try to reason, though, that she must have wanted it real bad, or she wouldn't have done it. So, within, I never got too disturbed! We lived at this address for a while when Lola confronted me and wanted to know why we were slipping away from each other. I was shocked to hear this, but it was important to hear for the sake of the marriage.

We sat down at the kitchen table and started to talk about it. Through this, I learned that both parties in a marriage have very important feelings. When the opposite party ignores those feelings, resentments begin and boil over to anger. Love goes out the window, and animosity starts to fester. So, it was important for me to re-evaluate my decisions and conclusions that were products of snap-judgments. We then agreed to listen to each other, consider each other and ponder any situation from every aspect. This agreement worked! We didn't always agree, but each was satisfied that consideration was used on each person's behalf. From then on, things ran very well. I admired Lola, for she made me feel very special as her husband. She would compliment me on my successes, and at times I thought she over-complimented too much, but that was better than none at all!

MORTGAGE

In the purchase of the house, we had a mortgage of $6,500 at 5%.

I like to pay cash, but you have to loan them money in a case like this, or you would never get anything of the necessity of material value. Lola had an aunt in Michigan who learned of our purchase and deplored that we had to pay interest. So she loaned us the $6,500, and we paid off the mortgage. After a while, Lola's Uncle Stanley died in Michigan and left her $6,500, which we promptly repaid to the Aunt who also lived in Michigan in Jackson's city.

BAKERY ROBBERY

I related earlier that we had the bakery, and I worked the store primarily in the evening. One evening the bell rang, which indicated there was a customer in the store. When no one was in the store, we would sit in the back of the house. As you entered the store from the house, there were three steps leading down into the store, which was set lower than the house. The register was right by the steps. As I stepped down, I could see that the situation was different.

Here was a younger guy with his hand inside his shirt, and it was obvious what he was about to do. He pulled out a loaded 32 and said, "This is a stick-up. Empty the cash register on the counter." I was a little afraid but very annoyed as well. There were thirty dollars in the register, and I laid it on the counter. I told him we were just trying to make a living, and he should stick up someone who had money.

This guy actually apologized and said, "I wouldn't be doing this if I didn't need the money!" He then told me to turn around and not move for thirty seconds. I turned around and jumped up the stairs, ran to the back of the house, and out the back door. There was a porch in the back that went right to the street. I ran across the porch and figured if he came running up, I would jump on him, but he was nowhere in sight. Years later, my brother Walter had a roofing business. He had a guy working for him that told him that he robbed a bakery with the same name Traska. Walter did not say anything because this guy asked him if we were related. Walter said something later to the police, and that guy went to jail.

TURNING IN A THIEF

I was downtown in Cleveland one afternoon. The area was in Ontario, and there was a post office there at one time. There was a man who was rolling a brand new tire down the street to his car. I checked the direction from which he came and saw a car trunk door with a neat round hole where the lock used to be. I took this guy's license number, and when a policeman came to my store, I told him about it and gave him the plate number. Sometime later, he said they watched this gang until they had all the evidence they needed and rounded up the whole gang! This incident happened forty years ago (1960), so it is safe to relate it now. Otherwise, if they had found out, I wouldn't be worth a nickel.

SAD TIMES

This comes to a most difficult period in this writing, and it is the start of a prolonged illness that took my wife, Lola. She came home one evening (1954) and said she felt strange. This feeling was the beginning of the Lupus that struck her down and eventually destroyed her kidneys. This illness lasted thirteen years and ended on Sept. 18, 1967.

After Lola's father's death, her mother's health started to slip. We took her in, but she complained so much, and it only burdened my wife to aggravate her condition. We had to place my mother-in-law in a nursing home. I had progressed in alcoholism and found it a good escape from the turmoil around me. Yet, I must emphasize that I blame no one for my drinking. I just liked it very much. For years, I performed my duties effectively but always felt that I should drink less. Lola's disease was diagnosed as nephritic (kidney) initially, and they said it would last six weeks.

They were wrong. A re-diagnosis was a couple of months later. This illness involved many hospitals: Mt. Sinai, St. Alexis, Marymount, Cleveland Clinic, back and forth over and over. We had two young girls: Susan and Marilyn, so I had my mother (Sophie1884 – 1973) help me out. Life was difficult running a bakery, providing a living, running to hospitals, and trying to be a father at the same time. Later it became more difficult because I got into AA and had to go to meetings to maintain my sobriety. My girls were deprived of a lot of time, but I tried my best to father them. My wife needed my support too, and at times I didn't know where to turn next. In the meantime, the bakery went downhill due to too much drinking, so I finally sold it and bailed out. Lola was in Mt. Sinai at this time, so I got a job there to be with her anytime I wanted and supported her.

VERY SAD TIMES

A lot could be said for the thirteen years of illness and the uncertainty of daily existing. It is very painful to dig it up. Nothing is pleasant about it, not the convulsions of the illness or the body full of water. The tube in her arm for dialysis would become blocked with clots of blood, and she had to be rushed to the hospital for emergency treatment. One night the shunt blocked up. It was one o'clock in the morning. We had to go to Mt. Sinai for treatment (the other side of downtown, E. 110th, and Euclid Avenue).

While almost there at E. 78th and Carnegie, a Black guy wearing a white shirt jumped out in front of my car. He tried to stop me, and I drove right at him. He sure jumped out of the way in a hurry. When I got to the hospital, I reported it to the police. They went out there and found he had stopped someone else, and they were lying on the street in the gutter in a pool of blood. They caught the guy.

One-time, Lola convulsed, and she was in danger of biting off her tongue. We had a wood stick for that but couldn't find it. I stuck my folded finger in her mouth instead and found out she had a good bite. So it went from day to day, and we didn't plan anything except to try to survive. Even my visits to the hospital were depressing from such frequency. Once again, I came to believe that there were no healthy women in the world, only sick ones!

LOLA'S ILLNESS AND MY SECURITY JOB

I would always try to tell positive things to the girls, but they were deprived of their mother, and it wasn't easy to put up a front. Lola would go on dialysis, and the after results always produced sore knees, vomiting, and a drained physical condition. One day, I saw the man who invented the kidney machine. What a wonderful man he was, and he said he always had time. We talked about Lola, and at the end of our conversation, he actually apologized that his machine wasn't better. The greater the man, the more humble they are. I'll always remember him!

Once I got the Security job, it was easier to see Lola, and it was a comfort to her. It was just four months before that I had been released from treatment from Charity Hospital and was in the process of recovery and withdrawal. (There will be another sheet that tells my treacherous journey through alcoholism). So when I got the job, it was good in one aspect, but not really good for a nervous alcoholic in the process of recovery. To add flavor to the situation, the times were unusual and turbulent since the riots were in process at that time. (Hough Riots July 1966 – civil disorder).

More interestingly, we were located in the heart of the area where they start! I didn't need to watch TV for excitement. I was living it! The newspapers always magnified the situation by reporting the riots, and from their accounts, it seemed like the whole city was in a riot. This was not so since riots were confined to localities. We, in Security, didn't feel too secure since we were outnumbered and didn't even carry guns, only clubs. The pay was $100 a week and uniforms supplied. It was a class establishment. The kind of work was a real learning experience, much different than a regular job. To wear a police uniform in those times was to travel at your own risk. They told us we are not policemen, but the badge said "Police," so you can guess what people concluded.

We had nighttime stake-outs in the dark parking lot, once there was a shoot-out in the Emergency Room, and I walked in the right after the action. My lieutenant said I was too late since he had to take the gun away from the assailant by himself. I really was not responsible for that since I was on a run of inspection. A run of that sort is a specific large section we cover by going to certain areas and punch a clock to show you were there. This was a big place, so there were four runs in all. That's why my run came through the Emergency Room. It was in the territory I was supposed to cover.

There was one run that covered a lot of hallways that only were occupied during the day. So the run at night was really weird and raised one's anticipation. All the people we met at that time were Black, and the mood at that time was hostile. This was when they called policemen "pigs." Walking the parking lot was an adventure for you never knew who had you I their rifle sights from the buildings nearby. There were other incidents, but you get the idea. Let's move on to other things.

Lola was released from the hospital and went to Mass at St. John's Church. There was a guy there named "little Joe." He kept telling Lola that he wanted to see me. This request got old, so I went down to see what he wanted...just to shut him up. He said he had a good job for me at St. John's. I worked for him part-time, and he liked my work. Now, I worked there while I was still drinking and messed up. The priest told me that if I did that again, I'd be fired, so I quit the job. Then I got the Security job at the hospital.

Now "little Joe" insisted that the priest wanted to see me too, so I went to see him. We had an interview, and the terms were $150 a week, $50 more than I was getting now. He said I should not do what I did before, and I didn't promise anything. Talk is cheap, and I was going to show him because I was sober now.

A few years after Lola died, I was still working at the church. Well, the priest had a sister named Marge. She worked part-time at the Rectory, and we used to talk occasionally. The time came when she mentioned her cousin, a widow whose husband had died six months before. I told her to tell me this six months from now when she had her head on straight (the new widow). In the meantime, I was occupied with a widow's club, and there were plenty of opportunities there.

I met many women there, and they all seemed to be well-heeled, but their attitudes seem different. Besides, I wasn't that old and still wanted to do something with my life. I will deviate now and give an account of my involvement with alcohol. Later, I will pick up the story and continue. This account must be told first because my feelings of self-worth became doubtful from drinking.

LOLA'S FINAL YEARS

To this point, I kept in sequence pretty well, but the part that changed my life was failing to report the passing of my wife, Lola. Perhaps I avoided it, but it must be told. It will be painful for me and some who read this, but I must tell it just how it happened. So we will postpone my report on my drinking and finish the account of this very, very sad and crushing death.

About six months before Lola passed away, Lola and I were summoned into a room with a group of doctors. That day they specifically told us that she would not survive this illness. This news was very hard to swallow, but they were being honest. Her condition went downhill from then on. Swelling from the water was common, plus the nervousness from the poisons. Her stomach was always upset, and we hung on a day at a time. One Sunday evening, I went to an AA meeting (I always cleared it with her if I should go). When I came home, her stomach was very upset. I gave her some antacids with a little bit of help. I sat with her, but about midnight, she told me to go lie down in the bed downstairs, so I did.

She said she would call me if she needed me. I got up early in the morning and looked into the room and knew that she had passed on. I regret so much that I missed being with her, but I don't feel guilty since she insisted, I lay down in bed. She was buried in a Franciscan Robe with a white rope around her waist. The funeral director told me she never had rigor mortis, and her body was as supple as alive. She passed away in September 1967.

MORTUARY

To further explain the statement, I made regarding Lola and her death, I add this note for verification of the source. The undertaker was Bill Bican, Sr. The first day I attended the funeral parlor to pay respects for my wife Lola (Sept. 1967), Bill came to me and asked if Lola had been extremely medicated. I said that she took the medicine prednisone. She had at times taken a pill to calm her down, but I am not aware of anything else. He told me the reason he was asking was that even in death, she never got stiff. He added that he had a hard time getting her positioned in the casket because the body was soft and supple like a live body. As she lay in her coffin in her St. Francis Robe (this was her request to be buried as a follower of St. Francis), she appeared to be more asleep than the other aspects a deceased body assumes.

You may draw your own conclusions, but I can assure you that she was a fine person who truly cared about people. God favors some of his people with incorrigibility of the body. To me, and this is only my personal and inner belief that perhaps she may be one of these in that category. This may be presumptuous on my part and be influenced by a large amount of emotionality and sentimentality, yet a part of me senses feasibility to such a thought. The reader can draw their conclusions, but I do pray that the reader's spirituality is enhanced by it!

MY INVOLVEMENT WITH ALCOHOL

I am back to my account of my progression into alcohol. No one plans it that way believe me, for it is an insidious disease that truly is cunning and baffling. I would drink a beer occasionally. A few shots at a wedding and would stop. When I started to work at the bakery, I found that a beer after work was a good relaxer. This routine went on for a while, and then one beer didn't do it anymore. Then it becomes two just to get that same glow. Well, after a while, two doesn't do it, and it becomes three. The beer in large quantities becomes too filling. When you drank a shot of whiskey, it added that extra kick. Soon beer becomes too filling, and whiskey is not. So, you give up the beer and stay with whiskey. Now the progression is the same, and you start consuming larger quantities.

Somewhere along the line, you realize that you might be drinking too much. You counter this by saying you can stop any time you want to, but you *don't* stop as you lull yourself with a false sense of complacency. The thing about alcohol drinking for that long a time will seem to calm and provide all your needs. Excessive alcohol, though, results in the hangover and the morning-after feeling. This never gets better, only worse. There is a time then that a social drinker turns into an alcoholic. When this happens, there is no change possible back to a social drinker. This last stage is deplorable since the ability to stop drinking is lost forever, and whether you want to or not, you continue to drink. There are no more choices left! Clinically, alcohol is listed as a poison, and excessive use results in brain damage or death. So I was hooked. My drinking had me trapped, I would have liked to stop, but I actually couldn't.

One afternoon in June, I was in the kitchen of the bakery shop. (This is the day I was married to Lola). I had just poured a drink out in a water glass. I didn't want to drink it, but it was the only way I could exist. As I sat at the kitchen table drinking and lamenting the fact, my mind took me back to my scalding as a child in the bakery shop. I recall my mother telling me that I was given up for dead since I wouldn't survive more than six hours. I remember my mother telling me how she fervently prayed to Jesus for me and how He let me live. It crossed my mind to ask HIM to help me overcome my alcoholism. I went into the bedroom, where a crucifix hung on the wall with Christ on it. Down on my knees, I went with a confession on my lips and a plea to God to help me again.

About four months later, toward evening, I was driving somewhere in the country. In the distance, I saw two sets of white "AA's on each side of the road! (**Frank had an illustration AA and on the other side of the road AA**) It was a miracle in itself, for the times I have seen such a sign is never or only once. Most unusual! At any rate, it was a sign from God for me to join AA (Editor's note: Alcoholics Anonymous). I drove between those signs, went home, and called AA. The man who helped me is called the sponsor. The man's wife was the one who bought my bakery. Those signs I saw had thoroughly convinced me that it was a sign from God, and I should go to an alcoholic hospital.

The alcoholism progressed to me having extremely abnormal fears, shakes, sweats, and hallucinations. My taste buds lost most taste, and my general condition was like being in hell. My breath would catch, and I couldn't breathe, and my heart palpitated. I had lost weight, and the general condition of my being had run down. I was put into Detox on a Saturday and was in the hospital for ten days! Those days are not easy to forget! They needed to be very impressive since I need to remember the lesson and the pain connected to the horrible experience. The hospital gives you a start to dry out, but there is a long, tedious road ahead on the way to sobriety! The mental pain now begins as the obsessions, compulsions, impulses, and urges overwhelm the sincerest intentions.

It is important to trust God that He will see you through this, give you the strength to bear the pain, patience to wait, sleeplessness, restlessness, irritability, and discontentment. All of this has to be surmounted by trusting God. It was my conviction that HE WOULD HELP ME DO THIS since he showed me the AA road signs and hung on! By myself, I was powerless and knew it! Well, they told me that when God's ready to release me, HE WOULD! It took a very long time with me, OVER THREE YEARS, but then God set me free. To this day (August 2000), I have been sober for over 33 years, and Nov. 1st will mark the 34th year. I know my writing on this subject has been very extensive, but I am telling you about me. You must remember that when Lola died, I had only sober for eleven months. The sorrow and pain engulfed me since I not only needed to stay sober but had two girls to look after!

LIFE AFTER LOLA

By this time, I had been working at St. John's Church. In my fragile state,

I had to put on an appearance of a strong front for my children, earn a living, maintain a home, be a father, and, most importantly, keep my sobriety. It was expedient that I go to AA meetings EVERY NIGHT and learn how to stay sober. The days were not easy, and my girls saw less of me than they should have, but I had to do what was necessary to remain sober. Drunkenness would have wiped out everything! There was much grief on my part, but I had NO GUILT about not doing enough for Lola. I did all I could!

Then the inevitable loneliness set in. It became very pronounced and very depressing. The widows club alleviated some of this, but it was like putting a band-aid on a wounded heart. By and large, the widows had raised their families and had a certain amount of bitterness that they had to do this alone. I saw this in each of them: some had loads of money, and all were well off. It seemed to me that if I married one of them, I'd be the odd man out. Their kids wouldn't accept me, and I'd always be the guy that their mother married.

Well, this takes me back to the priest's sister, Marge. She was Father Paul's sister who worked part-time at the Rectory. She is the one who mentioned her cousin, Rita, who was a widow. The first time Marge mentioned this was when Rita had been a widow for six months. That is when I told Marge to come back and tell me about it when she was a widow for at least a year.

RITA

No one can get their heads on straight in a half of a year.

About a year later, Marge mentioned it again. This time, I got the phone number and called her there. She had seven kids, ranging in age. We went out together a few times and had a lot in common. We made a Cursillo – which is a Spanish-type retreat but more intensive. (highly structured weekend Thurs-Sun retreats. Place a strong emphasis on community and evangelization/help Christians to become more fully Christian.)

The main point was though that she had that certain attraction that got my attention. Yet, here was a situation similar to the other situations that I sought to avoid. For there were older kids here too that most likely might not accept me. Then, I had my own girls to consider; how would they accept it? Those were my thoughts even before my intentions became serious.

The deciding factor was that she had two small boys who could use a father. My feelings always were that if I, as a little boy, lost my father, I would like some other man to marry my mother and be my father. They seemed to be nice children, weren't rich and flooded with possessions, and were of the same ethnic background. I must emphasize that I wasn't entirely generous and magnanimous, and my first cause was to fill that hole in my heart called loneliness! Knowing full well that this was a calculated risk for the both of us, we decided to marry.

Now there are many marriages between just one man and one woman with no children or complications that simply don't work out, and they divorce. Others with children fall apart and divorce too. I was aware of all this, and the complications of two families merging together would be difficult on both sides. Now we are dealing with various interpretations, feelings, anger, and personalities that need to blend into a working unit... into a family. This, in my opinion, has at least worked to perhaps better than I expected. There are other members of the family who I am sure will disagree with my opinion. I accept that as one would expect that nothing works perfectly.

Those who may feel abandoned; for this, I am deeply sorry. Some, as children, were good observers but made poor interpretations. Some carried these views for a long time and believed them. I am sure they caused a great deal of pain, and this I regret. As for myself, I did as well as I could, and not being perfect and made my share of mistakes. Yet, I feel that I had become useful and remained useful and contributed to the betterment of society.

This marriage has survived over thirty years. As I see it, we are a family, and I pray each day that each family member works together to make it a closer family. This is idealistic, but everyone has ideas of one sort or another.

This is as far as I will write, for my fingers hurt, and at age 80, I tire more easily.

These are pages called additions that I hope you find interesting. I left out discussing some personal aspects, but I assure you, I am perfectly human! Once again, I hope that the reader doesn't get bored!

Various Topics:

FAITH OFFERING

In some of these additions, there may be some repetition of the auto-biography itself. It is hard to remember all that I wrote, yet all true and accurate. I would rather repeat, though, than omit, so here goes. During Lola's illness, I was covered with Blue Cross and also had Traveler's Insurance. Despite all of this, the expenses started to exceed the coverage. The deficit was always paid in cash by me, but there came a time that all cash ran out. Then, the bills piled up to $3,500 and growing, a huge debt at this time.

Though that money was secondary to me, you must know that life has always been first in my mind. The new school at St. John's had been built (the 1950s), and each parishioner was assessed $250 to pay for the school. They sent me a bill for this amount. I had $300 cash to my name. The thought came to me to make a faith offering to the church of the entire amount, so God would help me out of this financial mess. Lola was not in favor of the idea, saying you don't make deals with God. Yet to me, this was not a deal. He knew my plight and could do anything according to His will. Fr. Liederbach was pastor at that time, and he saw Lola's side, but I insisted he take the $300, which he did.

The bottom line is that I kept up with my bills from then on, and at the end of a year, I had $3,000 in the bank! Take this for what you believe; I did mine by faith. I can just tell the facts the way it came about; it happened, so I tell it! I don't want to influence anyone by this; use your own conscience!

ARMY WAYS

Military service is and never should be confused with the life we lead as civilians. Sometimes things are done for purposes to make discipline a reality. A well-trained service person will respond to commands by being trained to do it. This could make a difference in combat whether he survives or not. It is important to develop an attitude in the soldier of a lingering sense of hostility. Some things are done to keep him angry; that is, in a subtle kind of way that he may not be aware of.

As punishment on occasion, I had a man dig a hole 8 feet x 8 feet and keep digging until he hit water. This punishment is illogical, but that was the order. He dug very deep then called me...water. I wasn't watching him, but I suspect some other soldiers helped him out, carried a lot of water, and poured it in the hole.

Then, there was a guy who really refused to be disciplined. His type usually gets court-martialed. When convicted, they are sent to the stockade, which is a marine prison. If he is rebellious there, he is placed in a hole 10 feet wide, 10 feet long, and 10 feet deep. He lives there, eats there, and sleeps there. If now there is *more* rebellion, a water hose is directed at him to cool him off. If he *continues* to rebel, the water keeps pouring in. Soon he realizes that if he doesn't shape up, he will be eating and sleeping in the water in the pit. His attitude changes through this. One man in my platoon went through this, but when he came back, he was the best soldier I ever had!

AA TROUBLED MEMBER
1985

To be as thorough as possible in my auto-biography, it is important that this AA activity be reported. It is an AA activity I participated in unexpectedly. There was a man in AA who had been in and out AA for the past twenty years. This man was full of rageful anger, so much in fact, that I thought he could explode. I prayed to God for him and said if he wanted me to help him, I was available. Sometime later, Sam Serio, the man full of anger, called me up and said he wanted to see me.

He was invited to come over, and we would talk. It was the month of May, and a beautiful day, so we sat in my backyard under my pear tree as he related his story. The gist of it was that he had a dream last night, and a celestial being advised him to call Frank Traska, and he would find help. Of course, I was willing, and through the grace of God, he has been sober ever since. This event must be at least 15 years ago! (around 1985) Now this fellow is a printer and has always been interested in publishing.

The next thing on his agenda was to start a small newspaper for AA's to read, which would carry a spiritual message. Out of the blue, he asked me to be the senior editor and write the column on spirituality. I was taken aback, but I accepted the challenge. The outcome was that I wrote an article every month for probably six years. The ideas would come after I asked the Holy

Spirit to tell me what to write. After that, the pen flowed! Thank God!

BOWLING

I have been recounting experiences of my life but have been remiss in listing my recreational activities. Every life needs activities of a pleasant diversion, and I am no exception to the rule. Some of my activities included football, baseball, ping pong, and bowling. Although I could not claim that my bowling was exceptional, there seemed to exist in me a faculty that caused me to run in streaks of high performance. My reliance was on these periods of "getting it together." Before long, it was very apparent to me that if I hit a streak, it would be possible to capitalize on it. Bowling establishments hold tournaments and pay good prizes for the one who posts good top scores. They also give a "spot" to the bowler according to his average.

My highest average ever was 171, and this only lasted one year. When I entered a tournament, I was assured a decent spot since we competed against some very stiff competition. One tournament was at the Bell Air Lanes in Fairlawn near Akron, Ohio. There were five games in this set across all the lanes across the whole line. This day I hit a real streak and averaged 215 actual, plus my spot. This was good for a prize of $750. The year before, this score would have won $2,500.

To list other successes, I'll mention a tournament in Sandusky in which I bowled top score with a 204 actual. This score paid $2,000. I won second place at a place in Fairview Park, which paid poorly. Then, three first places at the Carousel Lanes ($125 per payoff) and a second-place finished at $75 each. Of course, there were many others where my performances were simply terrible. It was a lot of fun, and I regret that it's over!

ART

In everyone's life, at some time or another, some occurrences may be termed unusual, odd, strange, coincidence, or other related terms carrying the same inferences. Yet, with a little more perusal, we may determine that the Lord Himself may have seen to it that it should work out that way.

The incident I write about, I believe, was a product of Divine intervention, if I may be that presumptuous. Let me relate the incident and the necessary background that precedes the evolvement in this period of my life. Years ago, I bought a wood-burning stove and scurried around collecting wood from all the available sources. One afternoon, as I drove on I-77 heading into Fleet Avenue, just before getting to Fleet, I glanced to my right into the wooded area and saw a tree that had fallen over.

Upon arrival at my home, I took my chain saw and headed back to the area of the fallen tree. The very first cut of this willow tree revealed a beautiful grain that really aroused my attention. The thought flashed into my mind to cut a few slabs of wood, sand them down, treat the wood to preserve it from splitting, and then coat it with clear varnish to enhance the beauty of the wood. I accomplished this, and the results were very satisfying. My wife, Rita, saw this wood and suggested to me to try to mount a picture on the slab. We had just had pictures taken of us to give to each member of the family. This was a great idea, and I had about thirteen slabs cut and started to prepare them all.

Once finished, I proceeded to make little frames for the pictures and mounted them. They looked good but seemed incomplete. I then decided to trim them with gold. My efforts were rather shabby initially, and I noticed that the last ones were better than the first, so *I did them all over again*. The second time around, my confidence level was high, so as I worked on the picture for my daughter Susan, I tried to paint a rose on it, and it came out fairly good. This, however, gave me confidence, and the thought flashed through my mind that if I could paint a rose, I could paint a picture.

My first attempts at this were really something else. It didn't discourage me, though, and kept at it. As I continued, I improved and improved. There is a particular joy in painting that gives an incentive to create. I continued to practice and to paint. One day at an AA meeting, a woman asked me if I could paint a winter scene for her, and how much would I charge for it? This request in itself started me on the thought of painting a picture for resale was out of my range. Instead, I said I would paint it, and if she didn't like it, don't buy it. The price was $125, and she said okay to that. I was shocked to ask it and shocked to hear she would pay it.

That was the start of my painting career. Others heard of it, ordered paintings, and the amount of sales has gone over $6,000. God finally led me into it by showing me the willow tree and awakening the sleeping artist within! Thank God for his tolerance and patience. Last month August 24,

2000, I entered an art show in Garfield Hts. A lady saw my painting and the name on it and said, "I always wanted a Traska!" I was fortunate to win two awards in a show in Independence, Ohio, winning first and third place, but my biggest joy comes from the good that can be done through my paintings! Thanks be to God!

ALCOHOLICS ANONYMOUS

I offer this version of my interpretations for those who are not familiar with the AA program. Anyone who has no need for the relief and help of Alcoholics Anonymous will quite possibly be very scant in knowledge or regard it as an organization of broken-down drunks, misfits, and total losers. This initial interpretation is not without credence or merit since a person who drinks must be a loser and realize it. This is the first requirement for a new member of AA. When the outsider continues to believe that AA houses total losers, they have lost the realistic rehabilitations that AA causes by the millions. To assert that AA is successful in every case would be ludicrous and ridiculous. AA is successful in the sense that the program will work *if* it is worked. Since there is a human factor, the human factor fails, not the principles of AA.

All of the above-written lines are factual, not a figment of imagination or views of any human opinion. The results speak for themselves, as miracles pile up in ever-increasing amounts! This sentiment is being written in gratitude for AA and in no way should be construed as a defense of this wonderful program. It is a personal witness since I have lived it and have seen the remarkable results in so many lives. We are asked to believe and trust in a power greater than ourselves. We came to believe because we become willing! Our old ways didn't work and only caused destruction and disgrace. As unbelievable as it seemed from the beginning, Alcoholics Anonymous worked if we worked it! It really will work; it really does!!! This summary certainly does not cover AA's miraculous accomplishments but should be a salute for many lives have been saved by it. I am happy to be associated with it and the privilege to participate in some of those miracles that God used as helpers. Long live AA!!!

OLD LADY

During the time we operated the bakery, we had a retail store. Business was never that good, but we did make a living at it. It, too, was an opportunity to meet people from various walks of life. There were well-cultured people, ethnicities, con-men, moochers, and the really poor.

One day, an old lady entered the store who was of Polish origin. She seemed poor with a coat that looked like fur with patches; her legs were wrapped with strips of nylon from old hosiery. There was a babushka on her straight hair; her face was worn and revealed her years' hardships.

She wanted to buy older bread and inquired about it. We were generous and helped those in need; we donated much pastry to Parmadale Orphanage. This lady seemed to need help, so I gave her bread free. She loved pumpernickel, and I gave what she asked for. Of course, she was grateful and expressed her thanks freely.

This went on for an extended period of time, and we got to know each other. At any rate, this is what I thought. One day, she took me into her confidence and revealed that she owned a four-family home on Frazee Avenue, had $16,000 in the bank, and wanted to will it to me. (Remember, this is in the 1960's when a car cost $6,000 new, and a loaf of bread cost 33 cents, and a dozen bakery 40 cents.) Well, this was a shock to me since my motivation was solely by scripture by Jesus, "Whatsoever you do to the least of my brothers, you do it unto me." The temptation was there, but I refused the offer.

I discovered that she was serious about this and insisted on saying that I had been better to her than any of her own family, better than a brother. My next offer was that we give it to St. Stanislaus Church. She wanted me to have it. After some convincing, she agreed, and I called the church. They said they would come down the next day. The next day no one showed up. They must have regarded this as a crank call for who gives away that kind of money or to will it that easily? This put up back to square one, and once again, I was it.

So, I called my accountant about it, and he said he could make out a Will. We were down there at the appointed time, and everything went according to plan! That is almost…now she wanted to leave her relatives in St. Louis a dollar apiece. I refused to be a part of this until she raised the amount to a more respectable number. I didn't want to be a part of that apparent snub and slap from the grave. So, the Will was completed, and I kept it in a metal box where her other valuables were kept. She had me hold this box in my possession.

Now, a short time later, she got sick. Some people took her in and convinced her that I was a con man who tricked her into the Will. Her name was Stella Poch, and one day she came to get the metal box back with all the possessions. She took the box but gave me the Will. They had cast doubt on my character, and I didn't like it. A short time later, she was sick again, and I went to see her with the Will. The Will was torn up in front of her and given back, and I quoted Pontius Pilate when he washed his hands of the matter. That was it, for shortly after, the lady passed on. The money went to a church on Broadway, to a church that says it is Catholic, but the priest can marry!

I needed to do what I had to do. For years ago, I read a passage that said, "Seek first the Kingdom of Heaven, and I will supply your needs!" I took that deal, and it hasn't failed yet, and it won't! Thanks to God!

BOILER INCIDENT

I worked at St. John's Nepomucene Church (3785 Independence Rd, off of Fleet Avenue) for seventeen years. This job consisted of many duties: cleaning, repairing, grass cutting, landscaping, heating, and air conditioning. Since bingo was played every Friday night, and still is to this writing, one of my duties was to clean up the hall afterward and the school on Saturday morning. This is mundane work and made for another ordinary day in the making. As previously mentioned, "Little Joe" worked at St. John's. So, this one morning, he met me in the hall and stated very calmly, there is something wrong with the church boiler. His calm manner suggested that matter was trivial, and it required no emergency activities.

We went into the church to see the heating units that the furnace sent the hot water to give off heat. Upon entering the church, the matter of urgency changed dramatically, for each register was hissing and snorting as it poured out hot steam with the vigor of Niagara Falls. We both had a sudden change in attitude and made haste into the basement to check the boiler. We saw a sight that made the blood run cold and the hair stand up on the back of the neck. This boiler was huge and generated a lot of heat, boiled a lot of water, and burned gas streams. The problem was that the gas control regulator had broken down, and gas in full force was pouring into the furnace. This caused all safety controls to keep popping off with hot live steam and became a veritable roaring tiger.

I ran behind the furnace to turn off the main valve of gas, for we were aware that there could be an explosion at any time! The valve was frozen open, and I told Little Joe to find something in a hurry for leverage to close the valve. Thank God he found a hollow pipe that fit over the handle of the valve and was able to pull the valve shut. What a relief this was as I pulled the safety valves to release the excessive steam. Right then, I said, let's get out of here in case there is some delayed action. The boiler was located right under the main church altar and would have wrecked it had it exploded.

Later, the plumber came and repaired the problem. He complimented Little Joe and me for a job well done. His very words were, "You guys sure had the presence of mind to stay and not run and did something about it!!! The church would have blown up!" Believe me; I wanted to run but stayed and admired Little Joe for sticking it out and not running out on me. This is the first time I am reporting this in detail. We told the boss about it (the Priest), but he never realized the gravity of the situation, and we didn't pursue it. Anyway, the church was saved from being damaged…not to mention our necks as well!

DREAM

The peculiarities of human nature at times cause us to believe the things we should doubt and to doubt the things we should believe. I admit that I subscribe to the category. Just today, I read an article by a well-educated man whose list of credentials verify this credibility. Still, his account in "Guide Posts" is so incredible that it taxes my imagination. (Norman Vincent Peale-inspirational content) He relates that he and his wife saw choirs of angels in the woods they were in and watched as they came and went.

Now that my skepticism has been expressed let me recount a dream I had that will undoubtedly raise a few eyebrows. Rita, my wife, was sick, bogged down by nagging congestion and that worn-out feeling from prolonged illness. We are in the Christmas season now, and it appears to be a dismal one, for the illness persists with no let-up in sight! That night I went to bed, and during the night, I had a dream. This dream was different, one of which I never had before or since. Here is the account: I was somewhere up in the sky with the surroundings presenting a rather light purple color suggesting the appearance of misty clouds. There, a Monk appeared before me in a grey habit and hood. The weave of the habit was coarse, and the hood dropped over his face in an inverted V-shape. This caused darkness on the area of the face. We stood close together, about two feet apart.

While standing there, I felt a current of exhilarating life flow from him to me. He transmitted a message to me that was not spoken but more by thought waves! The gist of the message was this, "we want you to know that God knows everything!" I knew he meant that God knew all things before, now, and after, and forever. Then he walked off a few feet and turned to me and said, "By the way, your wife is really sick, so when you get up, start boiling lots of water and keep soaking her feet until she is full of perspiration, and tomorrow she will be well!" When I got up, I was bursting with life and bubbling over with zest.

My wife wondered how I could be that cheerful when she was so sick! I told her about the dream, and when I got back from church, I would soak her feet, and she would be well the next day because the Monk said so. I didn't ask her sentiments as to my exuberance. They had to be doubtful at best! Bottom-lines pay off, though, since I did as I was told to do. And the following day, she was completely well! Not only did this happen, but it also carried its own verification!!!

TO BE READ LAST:
A Summary of this Life
The year 2000

AS I SEE IT

The preceding pages indicate that a lot can happen in life and does. Life seems to be everything that happens to you while one plans something else. At times, life seemed very worthwhile, and other times comes out mundane. There are very critical moments, moments of despair, moments of joy, times to ponder, to regret, repent, time to be happy, and a time to grieve. The reader could add their own list to this. How many times has mankind pondered the reason for it all? The evidence all around us indicates that there is a guiding power in charge; it could be no other way! This power gives every indication that His only interest is that life flourishes in abundance.

The earth is flooded with life of every kind. There are birds of every species and color, all types of animals of various descriptions, all types of bugs, and so forth and so on. All methods and varieties of methods are provided to sustain this life. We, as humans, are the most endowed, flooded with gifts of sight, feel, taste, hearing, and smell. Each person is given the capacity to love if we so seek it. There are options to not love, but the opposite generates resentments, hatred, vindictiveness, and rage.

We have a choice by free will, but the way we measure seems to come back to us. We all will experience things such as this since human make-up is very complex. The Creator of Life sent us a message in the form of a man: Jesus Christ, by name. To study the message that this God-Man brings is to study life itself. Yet, his words ring sharp and true and has attracted billions of people. I am one of those people and a follower who gets lost, stumbles, but keeps trying. This message, I am convinced, is the total of the meaning of life! Without Jesus, life would be pure folly! God bless all of you!

Frank Traska

www.ingramcontent.com/pod-product-compliance
Lightning Source LLC
LaVergne TN
LVHW051409080426

835508LV00022B/2996